HOW PSYCHOLOGY
APPLIES TO EVERYDAY LIFE

HOW PSYCHOLOGY APPLIES TO EVERYDAY LIFE

Charles I. Brooks and Michael A. Church

GREENWOOD PRESS
Westport, Connecticut • London

Library of Congress Cataloging-in-Publication Data

Brooks, Charles I., 1994–
    How psychology applies to everyday life / Charles I. Brooks and Michael A. Church.
        p. cm.
    Includes bibliographical references and index.
    ISBN 978-0-313-36486-0 (alk. paper)
    1. Psychology—Popular Works. 2. Psychology—Miscellanea.
3. Psychology—Textbooks. I. Church, Michael A., 1947– II. Title.
    BF145.B76 2009
    158—dc22   2008032945

British Library Cataloguing in Publication Data is available.

Library of Congress Catalog Card Number: 2008032945
ISBN: 978-0-313-36486-0

First published in 2009

Greenwood Press, 88 Post Road West, Westport, CT 06881
An imprint of Greenwood Publishing Group, Inc.
www.greenwood.com

Printed in the United States of America

The paper used in this book complies with the
Permanent Paper Standard issued by the National
Information Standards Organization (Z39.48-1984).

10 9 8 7 6 5 4 3 2 1

I dedicate this book to my wife, Joyce—*Charles I. Brooks*

To my wonderful wife, Nelya, who continues to support all of my endeavors, including this one—*Michael A. Church*

CONTENTS

PREFACE

As teachers we find that many students have difficulty doing a literature review on a topic. The availability of search engines and large databases can discourage students from narrowing their topic to something that will result in manageable output from electronic sources. For instance, a student interested in reviewing research comparing the effectiveness of antidepressant medication versus counseling when treating depression might enter ''depression treatments'' as a search phrase. The resulting output can be hundreds of studies, and the student is overwhelmed.

How Psychology Applies to Everyday Life provides students with a different strategy. We have formed 53 questions about human behavior, questions common to everyday living, such as ''Are pets good for our health?'' ''Should we hide our weaknesses from others?'' ''Does stress in the mother during pregnancy harm the fetus?'' ''Does serving size of food affect how much we eat?'' Then we describe and analyze a recently published study that offers a simple yes/no answer to the question.

Many readers may wish to go no further; they have learned something about 53 questions related to some aspect of human behavior. Students, however, may be researching the topic for a formal paper, and they may wish to look further into the topic. For them, we provide additional references and suggest how a question can be expanded.

Finally, we include a section with six questions about clinical practice. In this section, which focuses on actual case studies from our files, we deal not so much with questions answered by published research, but with questions answered by clinical experience with clients. We deal with misconceptions about what goes on in counseling and psychotherapy, the use of medications for psychological problems, and, when trying to help people, whether it is appropriate to focus on ''why'' they do what they do.

As a reference work, *How Psychology Applies to Everyday Life* is both a source of information on a psychological topic and a portal guiding the reader to further study on that topic. We have also found that *How Psychology Applies to Everyday Life* can be used as a text in a course on ''Current Issues in Psychology'' and as supplementary reading for a course in general psychology.

ACKNOWLEDGMENTS

We thank the following people who provided us with assistance at various stages in the preparation of this book: Diane Basta, Brian Blight, Kaitlyn Fiorino, Andrea Hochstuhl, Jess Kohlert, Reanna Lachner, and Heidi Pierson.

Charles I. Brooks
Michael A. Church
King's College
Wilkes-Barre, PA 18711
June, 2008

AUTHORS' WELCOME

Everyone is a psychologist! We all wonder why people do the things they do. How many times have you been in a group discussing the affairs of the world when the subject turns to the behavior of others?

- "Did you hear about Kenny's folks? They're getting a divorce! I wonder what went wrong? They seemed like such a happy couple. I wonder how the whole thing will affect Kenny?"
- "Did you hear about Susan? She's hooking up with Jen! Geez, what's with that? I know she's dated a bunch of guys!"
- "Did you hear about Joe's mom? Skin cancer! They caught it early and should be able to cure it, but how is that stress going to affect Joe?"
- "Did you hear about Wally? He's in AA sessions. Finally! Wasn't his dad an alcoholic? Wow! I wonder if Wally's kids will be drunks, too?"
- "Did you hear about Jane? She's all depressed and doing lousy in school. Her mom took her to the doctor for some Zoloft. Hell, I heard that stuff will make her commit suicide!"

A lot of us love to get into conversations like those above because they give us a chance to expound on our pet psychological theories about behavior. The problem is, when we're talking like that, we usually begin with a comment like, "You know what I think? I think …," Unfortunately, a lot of people could give a cat's whisker what we think! In fact, they would rather have us listen to what *they* think!

Sometimes these questions also catch your attention as students when you are faced with an assignment about some psychological issue. In this case you might be asked to review psychological literature and report on any one of a variety of topics that explain why we behave the way we do. For instance, you might be asked to find research that deals with post-traumatic stress disorder and why so many soldiers returning from Iraq seem to suffer psychological problems. You go to the library, log in to a standard psychology search engine like psycINFO, type in "post-traumatic stress disorder," and wait. What follows is a listing of sources that can number in the thousands! What do you do now? How do you sort through this huge mass of information and select articles that may be relevant to what you're looking for?

When confronted with such a situation, this book may help you long before you attempt to use the search engines. This book can give you a doorway, a first step in finding information on a specific topic. To give you that first step, we do not provide you with a comprehensive analysis of the topics covered. Rather, we focus on a specific aspect of a question about behavior, such as, "How does serving size influence how much a person eats?" A question is posed, a simple answer is given, and a single research study is described to explain how that answer was reached. Should you want to go further in your investigation, we give you accessible references specific to the topic to make your next steps more efficient.

How did we pick our topics? First of all, this is a book about what's going on in the world of psychology with respect to everyday questions. The focus is on questions we ask each other quite a bit, questions like, "Does playing violent video games lead to violent behavior?"; "Is marriage good for us?"; "Does spanking children make them unstable?"; "Do other racial groups all look the same?"; "Can the alcoholic drink socially?"; "Do children raised by gay parents turn out OK?"; "Are eyewitness accounts accurate?"; Is winter a cause of depression?"; "Does cell phone use compromise driving ability?"; "Does immediate counseling following a trauma prevent post-traumatic stress disorder?" Psychologists regularly publish research on these and other interesting questions, but students often miss the results because of the sheer volume of information that is available on the standard search engines. Consequently, it becomes difficult for you to sort through that information and focus your questions on specific aspects of an issue. We hope this book gives you that focus.

We try to keep the book upbeat and lighthearted. Many of the topics involve serious issues, but we want you to smile now and then while reading this book and to have fun with it. In fact, as we write, we picture you in class discussing an issue, thinking about an assignment you must prepare, or perhaps we see you in a dorm room or cafeteria with friends discussing why a particular person behaves a certain way. Many of these topics and conversations are quite serious: "There goes John. I hear he was told he should get alcohol counseling because he's already an alcoholic. I wonder if John or any alcoholic can ever drink socially?" Other topics are not so serious. "I told Ralph the keg was Bud Lite so he would drink it and not complain. It worked! He's drinking Miller, but he thinks it's Bud. I wonder if that works with most people?" Others are somewhere in-between. "Did you hear Janet went to a hypnotist to lose weight? I wonder if she's wasting her time and money?"

For each of our topics, we focus on a recent research article, something published in a legitimate professional psychology journal since 2000. We try to describe the results in straightforward, understandable, nontechnical language. We chose research that presents answers to basic, timely, and interesting questions about human behavior, questions like those we mentioned above. We think these questions are fairly common ones that pop up often in our daily lives and in discussions with others.

Be forewarned! When it comes to psychology and human behavior, straightforward and clear answers run the risk of being oversimplified! In fact, it is somewhat simplistic to ask a question like, "Will a male alcoholic have a son who becomes an alcoholic?" The best answer to that question is probably, "Well ... it depends." Answering the question precisely requires more information about the son's family life with mom and any brothers and sisters, his neighborhood and friends, his success in school, and a host of other things. To help you uncover some of the complexities of the topics in this book, we provide additional references. Now and then we will note the complications that can cloud an issue, but we don't get hung up on those complications; we'll just remind you that no one study provides the complete answer to an issue, and we'll provide you with the resources to delve deeper into the topic should you wish to do so.

No matter what our topic, we restrict ourselves to real results from published studies; whether we are giving the simple answer or pointing out complexities, we base our comments on research from reputable professional journals and books. So, whether you are preparing a paper or simply discussing the issue with others, the information in this book will allow you to say truthfully, "Recent research shows...."

The last section of this book deals with the practice of clinical psychology and will deviate a bit from the "published research" model we use in the other sections. The clinical section, which we call "Notes from the Shrink," presents real case studies, raises questions, offers possible interpretations concerning the case, and shows how psychological principles can be applied in the clinical area. The research sections of this book illustrate how psychologists investigate questions using scientific methodology; in contrast, the clinical section gives you a feel for how clinical psychologists go about their task of observing, assessing, and interpreting behavior. We hope the material in this section can help broaden your thinking about issues like depression, anxiety, personality disorders, and other psychological problems. We also hope this material can give you a better perspective when you discuss the behavior of those around you with your friends. Finally, we hope the clinical material can be a help to you in preparing formal reports on topics dealing with real-life problems.

PART ONE

SEX, BOOZE, AND OTHER FUN THINGS

1
Do Humans Prefer Curved Objects?

Men have a wonderful nonverbal way of communicating to other men that a particular woman is an eyeful: raised eyebrows, a heavy sigh, a tilt of the head, and, most crucial, making the outline of a curved shape with both hands. These signals all say, this gal is a glorious sight.

Curves on a female body are enticing to most men. Come to think of it, a lot of curved objects are attractive. Most car designs involve gentle curvatures. Angular exceptions like the Hummer seem to have a market, but they are also more likely to get highly negative reactions from many people. Take a look at the furniture at work and compare it with your home stuff. Office furniture, even when it's in a lobby, tends to be more angular, suggesting a formal, no-nonsense approach; home furnishings, on the other hand, are usually more curved, conveying relaxation and informality.

QUESTION: *Do we show more liking for curved objects than for sharp, angular objects?*
RESEARCH ANSWER: *Yes.*

ANALYSIS

Moshe Bar and Naital Neta of Harvard Medical School had fourteen subjects look at 280 pairs of objects. Half of the pairs were real objects, and the other half were meaningless patterns. Whether real or not, the objects in each pair were matched for various visual features except one: curvature; one member of each pair had sharp corners, the other member had curves. For instance, one comparison showed two wristwatches, one rectangular and the other circular. The objects were presented side by side very briefly (for about eight-tenths of a second) on a screen, and the subjects had to indicate which of the two they liked more, based on a simple "gut" reaction. The results were quite clear: Whether the objects were real or meaningless, the subjects showed a preference for the curved ones.

One very important thing to note here is that the time allowed to reach a judgment was very short, less than one second. Thus, the participants were not lingering over the pictures and thinking about their preference. Think about this aspect of the procedure. Were they to do so, the effects of experience could enter into the picture and confound the results a bit. With the short response time, however, we get a purer, more gut-level liking or disliking of each object.

The authors believe that we like sharp, angular objects less because they convey a sense of threat (e.g., arrows and knives). Whatever the reason, shapes do indeed seem to influence our impressions of objects and of people as well. "He's such a square" conveys a negative evaluation, whereas "He's very well-rounded" is a definite compliment. Be careful, though. A "square, angular" jaw on a man is usually seen as indicating decisiveness, independence, and assertiveness. Media reports often described Mitt Romney, one of the early candidates for the 2008 Republican nomination for president, in very positive terms, referring to his forceful, angular facial features. (Those features, however, were not enough to get him the nomination!) By the same token, in a job interview, that feature might work to your advantage if the employer is looking for a decisive leader. If, however, the employer is looking for a loyal worker to carry out the supervisor's policies without question, the angular feature might not be so helpful to you. And then there's that round, baby-face with the cutesy round eyes! Those features are great for an infant, but not so great for the 25-year-old interviewing with an employer looking for an aggressive go-getter with leadership potential.

Are shapes the *primary* determinants of how we think and react? Of course not. We can, however, certainly use the information about the influence of shape to our advantage. If you have angular facial features, it might be to your advantage to display well-rounded and cooperative behaviors; by the same token, if you have that cutesy, round baby-face, make sure you develop assertive and authoritative traits.

These comments raise some interesting research possibilities and something you can look for if you choose to investigate this topic further. That is, you might ask yourself if the types of behaviors one displays can outweigh their facial features. Both of these factors can be varied in a research investigation. For instance, if participants observe two people behaving assertively, but one has angular facial features and the other has rounded features, will the observers rate the effectiveness of the people differently?

PRIMARY REFERENCE

Bar, M., and M. Neta. 2006. Humans prefer curved visual objects. *Psychological Science* 17: 645–48.

ADDITIONAL REFERENCES

Demirbilek, O., and B. Sener. 2003. Product design, semantics and emotional response. *Ergonomics* 46: 1346–60.

Leder, H., and C. Carbon. 2005. Dimensions in appreciation of car interior design. *Applied Cognitive Psychology* 19: 603–18.

Reber, R., N. Schwarz, and P. Winkielman. 2004. Processing fluency and aesthetic pleasure: Is beauty in the perceiver's processing experience? *Personality and Social Psychology Review* 8: 364–82.

2
Is Beauty in the Nose of the Smeller?

It's not unusual to hear someone say, "I could smell him coming a mile away"; or "I smell a rat!" No matter what the context of these comments, the message is clear: We humans put a lot of faith in our sense of smell! But here's a question for you.

QUESTION: *Does body odor influence our attraction to someone else?* Now we're not talking about being repulsed by someone who just came out of the gym after a rigorous four-day workout! We're talking about more subtle influences of body odor on how attractive we might find someone.

RESEARCH ANSWER: *Yes.*

ANALYSIS

Yolanda Martins and associates, researchers at the Monell Chemical Senses Center in Philadelphia, Pennsylvania, collected odor samples from four groups: heterosexual males and females, homosexual males, and lesbians. Body odors were collected after a careful nine-day procedure. During this time, donors washed with odorless soaps and shampoo, did not shave their armpits, and did not eat

certain items like garlic, known to affect body odor. The donors were, so to speak, "washed out." Then the donors wore cotton pads in their armpits daily for three days, changing pads each day. The used pads were placed in an odorless plastic bottle with a flip lid. These bottles were subsequently given to the research participants who placed the bottle under their noses, raised the lid, took a good whiff, and then closed the lid. When they took the whiff, of course, they had no idea where the scent came from. They were simply asked to rate the scent on a pleasant–unpleasant scale.

Among the findings: heterosexual males, heterosexual females, and lesbians preferred odors from heterosexual males to odors from gay males. Gay males, on the other hand, preferred odors from gay males. Gay males also had a greater preference for odors from heterosexual females than from heterosexual males.

There were a variety of other findings but you get the point: both gender and sexual orientation had an influence on body odor preference. It appears, therefore, that natural body odor plays a role in social recognition and preference. (We don't know what to tell you if you're conveying this information at lunch and some of your friends begin backing away from you!)

When thinking about these results, it's important to remember the context of this particular study: sexual orientation. We're sure you can come up with many other applications, as well as possible research ideas, to see how odor may apply to various social situations other than sexual orientation.

PRIMARY REFERENCE

Martins, Y., G. Preti, C. R. Crabtree, T. Runyan, A. A. Vainius, and C. J. Wysocki. 2005. Preference for human body odor is influenced by gender and sexual orientation. *Psychological Science* 16: 694–701.

ADDITIONAL REFERENCES

Jacob, S., M. K. McClintock, B. Zelano, and C. Ober. 2002. Paternally inherited HLA alleles are associated with women's choice of male odor. *Nature Genetics* 30: 175–79.

Ober, C., L. R. Weitkamp, and N. Cox. 1999. HLA and mate choice. In *Advances in Chemical Signals in Vertebrates, 8th ed.,* edited by R. E. Johnston, D. Müller-Schwarze, and P. Sorenson (189–99). New York: Plenum Press.

Preti, G., and C. J. Wysocki. 1999. Human pheromones: Releasers or primers—fact or myth. In *Advances in Chemical Signals in Vertebrates, 8th ed.,* edited by R. E. Johnston, D. Müller-Schwarze, and P. Sorenson (315–31). New York: Plenum Press.

Preti, G., C. J. Wysocki, K. T. Barnhart, S. J. Sondheimer, and J. J. Leyden. 2003. Male axillary extracts contain pheromones that affect pulsatile secretion of luteinizing hormone and mood in female recipients. *Biology of Reproduction* 68: 2107–13.

Savic, I., H. Berglund, and P. Lindström. 2005. Brain response to putative pheromones in homosexual men. *Proceedings of the National Academy of Sciences, USA:* 102: 7356–61.

3
How Quickly Do We Form Impressions?

It's certainly no secret that we evaluate people according to how they look. But how long does this evaluation process take? Seconds? Minutes? Hours? When most of us talk about our first impressions of someone we met, we usually stress how quickly the impression was formed. Nearly ten years ago, for instance, we were involved in interviewing candidates for a job. There was an instance when a candidate walked into the interview room, and one of us felt an immediate dislike of the person. By immediate, we mean seconds.

"The person walked in the room and even before shaking hands I found myself saying silently, 'Go away! I hate you! I wouldn't hire you if you were the last person on earth!'" (The person didn't get the job in this case. None of the four interviewers liked the candidate.)

First impressions are real, and, of course, they may turn out to be correct or horribly inaccurate. Most of us know someone who has a close friend or significant other "I couldn't stand" upon the first encounter. But in this section we're not interested in whether first impressions are made quickly; they are. We want to know how quickly.

QUESTION: *Can a first impression be made in one second or less?*
RESEARCH ANSWER: *Yes.*

ANALYSIS

Janine Willis and Alexander Todorov of Princeton University collected a bunch of pictures of people and standardized them (such things as size of photo, color, manner of dress, head shots only, and neutral expressions). Then they had evaluators look at the pictures and judge the people in the pictures on characteristics such as honesty, likeability, attractiveness, and aggressiveness. Those pictures that showed some consistency in traits across evaluators were chosen for use in subsequent experiments.

In the experiments, the researchers asked if research participants could make fairly accurate judgments of traits when a photograph of a person was presented for as little as one-tenth of a second. Here's the setup. Imagine you are sitting in front of a computer screen and a picture of a face flashes for one-tenth of a second. Other observers, who have looked at the picture for a much longer length of time, have agreed that this person is attractive. Will you agree with those observers, even though you only see the photo for a tenth of a second? Apparently so! The photographs were shown to participants at a set position on a screen, and even when the exposure time was only one-tenth of a second, they made judgments about that person's traits (like honesty, likeability, and attractiveness) that were extremely close to the judgments made by people who had lots of time to look at the picture. In other words, the first impression took only milliseconds to form!

Obviously, as we spend time with a person, our initial and quick inferences and attributions about them can change drastically. But one thing seems certain: first impressions based on facial appearance take place extremely quickly. So here's a new line for desperate men: "Such is your beauty that mere milliseconds were all I needed to be attracted to you!"

The study we describe in this section is consistent with other research described in the popular recent book, *Blink*, by Malcolm Gladwell. A first impression is not the only behavior that occurs in "the blink of an eye."

PRIMARY REFERENCE

Willis, J., and A. Todorov, A. 2006. First impressions: Making up your mind after a 100-ms exposure to a face. *Psychological Science* 17: 592–98.

ADDITIONAL REFERENCES

Gladwell, M. 2005. *Blink: The Power of Thinking Without Thinking.* New York: Little, Brown, and Company.

Grill-Spector, K., and N. Kanwisher. 2005. Visual recognition: As soon as you know it is there, you know what it is. *Psychological Science* 16: 152–60.

Todorov, A., A. N. Mandisodza, A. Goren, and C. C. Hall. 2005. Inferences of competence from faces predict election outcomes. *Science* 308: 1623–26.

Todorov, A., and J. S. Uleman. 2003. The efficiency of binding spontaneous trait inferences to actors' faces. *Journal of Experimental Social Psychology* 39: 549–62.

4
Is Writing Good for Our Health?

You may know someone who keeps a daily diary. Usually, we don't think much about diaries because they typically involve just reporting on a day's activities and events. We bet, however, many of you have felt hurt or angry, sat down and wrote about it, and almost miraculously felt better about things—maybe not right away, but often the very next day.

Check this phenomenon out with your parents. If they're over 50, no doubt many years ago they endured the "we've got to talk" session with a "significant other," felt crushed and unworthy after the experience, and proceeded to write a letter to this "now-hated other" later that night. This letter, of course, would fit the category, "You-are-the-scumbag-of-the-earth." (The reason we restrict this story to the over-50 crowd is so we don't have them sitting down at the computer.)

By the time they finished writing, it was pretty late, so they put the letter aside to be mailed the next day. Of course, when they reread the letter by the light of a new day, it just didn't sound as good, or seem to be such a good idea. So they chuckled a bit and tore it up, feeling better and perhaps a little wiser. (Note that

you are in a more precarious position than your parents, because upon finishing the letter—an e-mail or text message, of course—it's easy to hit the "send" button! Bad move! At 2 A.M., after writing a "You-are-the-scumbag-of-the-earth" e-mail, always hit "save," not "send.")

But back to our letter. Our point is, your parents will likely say they really did seem to feel a little better after writing it. Maybe the effect did not occur overnight, and maybe it took several writing sessions, but putting their feelings down on paper seemed to have a therapeutic effect. So what about it? Is there any good scientific evidence for such a positive effect?

QUESTION: *When we are emotionally wound tight, does it help to write about how we feel?*
RESEARCH ANSWER: *Yes.*

ANALYSIS

Joshua Smyth and his colleagues at the State University of New York at Stony Brook have done a series of studies on the effect of writing about personal traumas on physical and psychological health. Examples of traumas include the breakup of a relationship, death of a loved one, or involvement in an accident. In Smyth's general procedure, people were asked to write about some personal trauma for a few minutes a day for several days. A control group of people was asked simply to write about the plans for the upcoming day.

After the writing period, the participants in the experiment were given both physical and psychological evaluations. The physical tests involved assessment of how well their immune system was functioning; the psychological evaluations involved asking the participants how effectively they felt they were meeting the stresses and challenges in their lives. On both measures—physical health/ immune system efficiency, and psychological strength for coping with the challenges of life—the group that wrote about personal issues scored better than the group that merely wrote about the upcoming day.

When we ask students to provide some explanation for these findings, most usually say there is some sort of energy release, getting rid of negative thoughts and feelings, "getting it off your chest," a cleansing of negative emotions that is responsible for the benefits of writing. The researchers, on the other hand, see another factor as responsible for their findings. They stress that writing about troublesome issues helps restructure our thinking. That is, as we write about things that are bothering us, we're actually dealing with conflicts at some intellectual and cognitive level; we're allowing ourselves to see things in a new perspective while thinking things through.

Expressive writing about things going on in our lives may also improve our relations with other people. For instance, Richard Slatcher and James Pennebaker of the University of Texas at Austin recruited people who were involved in a committed romantic relationship. In the study, the participants were asked to write for three consecutive days for 20 minutes each day, about their deepest thoughts and feelings concerning their relationship. They were not writing to their loved one; they were writing "to themselves," reflecting on how they felt about the relationship. Another group of participants simply wrote about their daily activities.

After this three-day period, the experimenters analyzed instant messaging (IM) communication for each of the couples in the study for the next few weeks (with permission, of course!). The results showed that, compared to the group that simply wrote about daily activities, the IMs of the people who previously wrote about their thoughts and feelings used more emotionally expressive words in the messages to their partner. Furthermore, they were more likely to still be dating their partner three months after the experiment than were participants in the other group.

In this case, we have a study showing that putting one's thoughts and feelings about a relationship down on paper actually influenced, for the better, the nature of communication with the partner. There was measurable improvement in the stability of the relationship.

Consider what these studies are saying: Put your thoughts down on paper; write down how you feel about emotional issues in your life, how you deal with them, and how you react to them. Doing so can potentially improve your physical health, increase your psychological stability, and enhance communication in your interpersonal relationships. If you're in a committed relationship, now might be a good time to take a break and IM or text your significant other. Share some positive things, such as, "I'm looking forward to having a good time with you this weekend." Even share some things that are bothering you, such as "I'm worried about the speech I have to give next week."

If you research this topic in more detail, you might keep in mind the common "release-of-emotion" explanation we noted earlier that students often give for the writing effect. Whereas getting things off our chests can be very therapeutic, such a process usually works in a context of helping us restructure our thinking about an issue. For instance, Judy may yell at Mary for forgetting to join her for a study session as planned; Judy says she's hurt that Mary would "blow her off" in such a way, especially when she told Mary she needed help with the material.

Mary says, "I was sitting in my room waiting for you to call and say you were ready to study. When you didn't call I figured you got hung up somewhere or were running late." For the next few minutes, they talk, and Judy is able to vent some of her frustration and hurt when she thought Mary was no longer interested in helping her. Judy may feel better in getting her frustration out, but the reason she feels better is because venting her emotions allows her to reconstruct her thinking that Mary had deserted her. The venting has allowed Judy to discover that she misinterpreted the situation, and Mary is still her friend.

PRIMARY REFERENCE

Slatcher, R. B. and J. W. Pennebaker. 2006. How do I love thee? Let me count the words. *Psychological Science* 1: 660–64.

ADDITIONAL REFERENCES

Butler, E. A., B. Egloff, R. H. Wilhelm, N. C. Smith, E. A. Erickson, and J. J. Gross. 2003. The social consequences of expressive suppression. *Emotion* 3: 48–67.

Gordon, K. C., D. H. Baucom, and D. K. Snyder. 2004. An integrative intervention for promoting recovery from extramarital affairs. *Journal of Marital and Family Therapy* 30: 213–31.

Lepore, S. J. and M. A. Greenberg. 2002. Mending broken hearts: Effects of expressive writing on mood, cognitive processing, social adjustment, and health following a relationship breakup. *Psychology and Health* 17: 547–60.

Lepore, S. J. and J. Smyth. 2002. *The Writing Cure.* Washington, DC: American Psychological Association.

5

What Is the Cost of Holding a Grudge?

The question we want to pose here has a lot to do with the previous section. There we noted the benefits of writing about our feelings, especially those involved in some traumatic event. The act of writing seems to help us restructure our thinking and feelings about events. In this section we want to take things a step further. What if those bothersome feelings involve holding a grudge?

We all get mistreated by others now and then. We get bullied, insulted, given a lousy grade, turned down for a job, fired, criticized by parents, or rejected by romantic interests. Such actions from others often lead us to think negatively about them, and we may carry a grudge or dislike for them in our minds for months, even years. We seem to live OK from day to day, but if we hear a certain name we think something like, "That SOB! I'll never forgive him for what he did to me. In fact, I find it comforting to imagine him staked naked to the ground covered in sweet syrup right next to a colony of killer ants!"

Many religions, of course, say it is appropriate to forgive others for their transgressions against us. In our everyday conversations, others also tell us it is not good to hold a grudge or refuse to forgive someone for something they did to us. It seems we usually agree with this warning because holding a grudge and not forgiving often seems to be a lot of hard work, and something that is really not a lot of fun to do. No matter what our mood, when the memory of a tormentor comes up, we just turn sour and get negative just thinking about it. On the other hand, forgiveness also requires a lot of work and energy. Let's face it, if you have a personal high-school bully who makes your life miserable on a daily basis for four years, finding it in your heart to forgive this person years later just might be more trouble than it's worth; plus, you figure, "the bastard at least deserves my everlasting anger, and if I ever see him again I'll tell him so." In this case, holding onto the grudge seems pretty harmless and just a part of our youthful memory structure.

QUESTION: *Psychologically speaking, is holding onto a grudge, or failing to forgive someone, relatively harmless?*
RESEARCH ANSWER: *No.*

ANALYSIS

Charlotte Witvliet and her colleagues at Hope College wired up some college students to measure their heart rate, blood pressure, skin moistness, and muscle tension, all good measures of emotionality. During a highly structured two-hour test session, the researchers then asked the students to think about a person who had done them some personal harm in the past, and whom they still blamed for the action. At various points during the testing, the students were asked to imagine themselves in a conversation, and either forgiving or not forgiving the person for the actions against them.

In the forgiving phases, the students were instructed to concentrate on having empathy for the person, trying to see things from a new perspective, and imagining various ways they could state their forgiveness. In the unforgiving phases, the students were told to remember the hurt they had felt in the past from this person, to rehearse the earlier negative events, and to restate the grudge and unforgiving feelings they had toward the person.

No matter what the measure of body arousal, all showed increased arousal during the unforgiving phases of the interview procedure. Furthermore, during these phases the students reported they felt more angry, more aroused and nervous, more sad, and less in control of their emotions. Thus, looking at both psychological and biological states, the unforgiving phases of the study seemed to put more of a strain on the subjects. Forgiveness, on the other hand, was a piece of cake; the subjects were more relaxed and understanding, and felt much better about being able to control their emotions.

This study only provides a window into what happens as a result of carrying a grudge or staying unforgiving toward someone else. Witvliet and her colleagues speculate, however, that holding a grudge over a long period of time may weaken our bodies, affect our immune system, and contribute to health problems. One thing for sure, holding grudges seems to make us more vulnerable to episodes of anger and other negative emotions. The really nice thing about the study described here is that the forgiveness apparently need only be imagined. The student who spread bad rumors about you and who got chosen (unfairly, of course) to assist the teacher in a research project is someone you want to hate for the rest of your life. But you now know the negative effects of holding onto this grudge. Remember, you don't have to meet with him and tell him all is forgiven; just imagine how you would do it, and then go on with your life. Forgive (in your mind, at least) and forget seems to be good advice!

PRIMARY REFERENCE

Witvliet, C. V., T. E. Ludwig and K. L. Vander Laan. 2001. Granting forgiveness or harboring grudges: Implications for emotion, physiology, and health. *Psychological Science* 12: 117–23.

ADDITIONAL REFERENCES

Enright, R. D., and C. T. Coyle. 1998. Researching the process model of forgiveness within psychological interventions. In *Dimensions of Forgiveness*, edited by E. L. Worthington, Jr., (139–61). Philadelphia: Templeton Foundation Press.

Freedman, S. R. and R. D. Enright. 1996. Forgiveness as an intervention goal with incest survivors. *Journal of Consulting and Clinical Psychology* 64: 983–92.

McCullough, M. E. and E. L. Worthington Jr. 1994. Encouraging clients to forgive people who have hurt them: Review, critique, and research prospectus. *Journal of Psychology and Theology* 22: 3–20.

Tennen, H. and G. Affleck. 1990. Blaming others for threatening events. *Psychological Bulletin* 108: 209–32.

Thoreson, C. E., A. H. S. Harris, and F. Luskin. 1999. Forgiveness and health: An unanswered question. In *Forgiveness: Theory Research, and Practice*, edited by M. E. McCullough, K. I. Pargament, and C. E. Thoresen (254–80). New York: Guilford Press.

6

Are Sex and Violence Good for Sales?

"Sex sells." Maybe you've heard that comment before. We associate it with Bob Guccione, who began *Penthouse*, many years ago. It's pretty obvious what Guccione is talking about: if you have a product you want people to buy, jazz it up with sex. Like Guccione, we know full well that for the past 50 years, young men have NOT bought *Playboy* for the sophisticated articles. And who is the genius responsible for bolstering sales of *Sports Illustrated* once a year by suggesting, "Let's have a swimsuit issue!"

In one of our psychology courses recently, we were discussing perception and the kinds of things that make objects more appealing. We raised a question, mostly directed at the men in the class: "Let's assume you had to choose between attending one of two movies, neither of which you knew anything about. One is rated PG, the other R. Solely on the basis of the ratings, which would you choose?" Well, surprise, surprise, R won hands down. The reason for the vote was not surprising either and was expressed rather eloquently by one young man: "The R movie is more likely to have sex and violence in it." We can only wonder if the violence really mattered in the vote!

In this section we want to present a slightly different angle to this issue of sex and violence. This different angle will give you a definite advantage in casual conversations, class discussion, or if you decide to do a formal paper on this topic.

QUESTION: *Will a product be more attractive if it's advertised in a TV program that contains sex and violence than if it's advertised in a program without sex and violence?*

RESEARCH ANSWER: *No*. Sex does not always sell!

ANALYSIS

At the University of Michigan, Brad Bushman had subjects watch TV shows that fell under one of four content categories: V (violence), S (sex), VS (both violence and sex), and neutral (no violence or sex). There were several shows for each category. An example of a V show was *24,* an S show was *Sex in the City*, a V + S show was *World Wrestling Entertainment RAW,* and a neutral show was *America's Funniest Animals.*

Bushman next assembled some TV ads for relatively unfamiliar products, items that are seldom seen advertised on TV (e.g., Libman Nitty Gritty Roller Mop, Natra Taste, and Nutra Nails). When the participants watched the taped TV show in a standardized setting, the original ads were removed and the new ads were inserted in their place. Thus, the show presentation was exactly as one would see it on TV except ads were changed.

After watching the shows, the viewers had to rate them according to how much sexual or violent content they had. This rating provided a check that the shows really did differ with respect to sex and violence. Then, without any prior notice, subjects were given extensive memory tests pertaining to the products in the ads that had been inserted into the show. The tests assessed whether they remembered the product, whether they would be likely to purchase that product, and whether they would select a coupon for that brand. The results were pretty interesting:

- Memory for products in shows *without* sex or violence was 68 percent higher than for shows with sex and violence.

- Viewers of shows *without* sex and violence were much more likely to recognize an advertised product than when it appeared in shows with sex and violence. Brand recognition was 51 percent higher in the former case.

- Viewers who watched shows *without* sex and violence chose 35 percent *more* of the products as "likely to buy" compared to when the products were in the sex/violent shows.

- Those who watched shows *without* sex and violence selected 33 percent *more* coupons for products than those who watched shows with the sex and violence.

It is important to note that the 336 participants in this study were 18 to 54 years old, and the age distribution was formed to be close to the actual distribution of TV viewers in America: 17 percent, ages 18–24; 12 percent, ages 25–29; 14 percent, ages 30–34; 15 percent, ages 35–39; 16 percent, ages 40–44; 14 percent, ages 45–49; 13 percent, ages 50–54. Thus, there is nothing in the composition of the sample that would lead us to question how representative the sample is of the typical American viewer. (This observation, by the way, raises an important issue when you are reviewing studies. Always be aware of the sample studied, and ask to what extent results from that sample can be generalized to other types of people.)

What's going on here? Can we reconcile this finding with that old adage, "sex sells"? We think so. Let's remember that the adage is in the context of selling a product using sex. If a product designed for men has a picture of a sexy girl on it, guys might be more likely to buy it than if it has no picture on it. The study we just looked at, however, is putting *non-sex content* ads in different types of shows. That is, if a TV show is "sexual content," and another is "great for the whole family," it's clear which one the typical 18-year-old guy might want to watch! But if you're a marketing executive and you choose to advertise your product designed for the 18-year-old in the sex-oriented show, you are probably wasting your money. Yes, he's watching the show, but unfortunately, your ad gets lost in the content of the show. He loves the show, but doesn't remember the ad too well. So what do you do? Hmmm. Let's put sex in the ad itself to counteract the effect! Doing so brings us back to the "sex sells" adage, and makes the show content less distracting to the ad content.

To sum up, if you want to increase viewership for a TV show, put more sex in it! Just remember, however, that advertising products in that sexy show will not be all that effective. Of course, you can counter that problem by simply putting some sex in your advertisement. That strategy may indeed sell your product (or at least make the viewer more likely to remember the ad). If you think, however, that putting a nonsexy ad in sexy shows will help sales, you may be on thin ice. The content of the sexy show itself will distract the viewer from the ad and reduce the effectiveness of the ad. Another possibility, of course, is that the sexy content of the show is so arousing that it interferes with the effective memory processing of an advertisement. In fact, the viewer may simply see the ad as a bothersome intrusion into an otherwise enjoyable show and thus tune out the ad.

How about violence? Our research question mentioned sex AND violence. Well, it turns out that violent TV shows are not good for selling products either. Brad Bushman and Colleen Phillips did an extensive review of studies of violent TV shows and how well viewers remembered the products that were advertised. They concluded that the evidence is pretty clear that televised violence greatly reduced memory for products advertised in those types of shows. The finding occurred for both men and women, and across viewers of all ages. Violence, like sex, is likely to arouse some strong emotions and involvement in the viewer. Suddenly switching mental gears when a commercial comes on is difficult, and thus the message of the ad gets lost. And, once again, of course, the viewer could also consider the ad an unwelcome intrusion into the emotional experience of the show.

It's quite possible, of course, that any TV show content producing strong emotional interest and arousal in the viewer will make advertisements less effective. That is, the content might not have to be sexy or violent to produce the same effect. Recently, one of us was watching a movie with his wife. The movie, a romantic comedy with morality messages mixed in and virtually no sex or violence, was 11 years old, one they really liked, and one they hadn't seen in some time.

> We really enjoyed seeing the movie again, and several times during the show we commented how we had forgotten that part of the movie. Seeing those scenes only increased our enjoyment. Every time an ad came on, however, we found ourselves quite irritated. Here we were, right in the middle of our enjoyment when, ZAP, another ad interrupted our pleasure. Needless to say, these ads, if we remembered them at all, were associated with irritation and displeasure, certainly not what the sponsors intended.

Advertising executives, of course, are well aware of these and other problems with trying to convey a product message to viewers. That awareness is probably one reason products and ads appear repeatedly in all types of shows. Eventually, viewers are worn down until, in true zombie-like fashion, they look at products on the shelf in the store, see one that looks familiar (they've seen it on TV thousands of times!), and reach for it. There is security in familiarity, and increasing familiarity is the ultimate selling strategy.

This topic is a great one for a research review because it illustrates a fundamental psychological truth when posing a question about human behavior: "It depends." That is, human behavior usually depends on a host of factors, and to predict the direction behavior will take requires us to know which of those factors is in play. In this book, we give you simple, straightforward answers uncovered in a representative research study. When you investigate the topic further, however, you will do well to look for those factors that make the ultimate answer to a research question, "It depends." Be prepared in your report, however, to answer the question, "It depends on *what?*"

PRIMARY REFERENCE
Bushman, B. J. 2005. Violence and sex in television programs do not sell products in advertisements. *Psychological Science* 16: 702–08.

ADDITIONAL REFERENCES
Bushman, B. J. 1998. Effects of television violence on memory of commercial messages. *Journal of Experimental Psychology: Applied* 4: 291–307.
Bushman, B. J. and L. R. Huesmann. 2001. Effects of televised violence on aggression. In *Handbook of Children and the Media*, edited by D. G. Singer and J. L. Singer (223–54). Newbury Park, CA: Sage.
Bushman, B. J. and C. M. Phillips. 2001. If the television program bleeds, memory for the advertisement recedes. *Current Directions in Psychological Science* 10: 43–47.

7

Can You Blame It on the Booze?

Next time you're talking to someone old enough, maybe a friend or a relative, and they are reminiscing about old times, or perhaps taking inventory of their mistakes in life, ask them how many of those mistakes can be traced to booze. It may be true that the good Lord protects fools and drunks, but the latter just survive to pay for mistakes. Many booze-related missteps, of course, seem to involve sex. We've heard it before: unprotected sex, rape, infidelity, wild sex at the office Christmas party, weekend parties—all sorts of regrettable sexual behavior that occur because folks were drunk and thus had their judgment blurred. It seems virtually everyone believes that alcohol, because it tends to remove sexual inhibitions, increases the likelihood that we will do stupid things, especially sexual things! It's just plain obvious that booze promotes risky sexual behavior. Right?

QUESTION: *Will alcohol intoxication automatically make someone engage in risky sexual behavior?*
RESEARCH ANSWER: *No.*

ANALYSIS

There is no doubt that booze and risky sexual behavior often go hand-in-hand. Any college administrator responsible for overseeing student life will confirm this observation. We have had numerous informal conversations with students seeking advice about various problems resulting from sexual indiscretions. The situation could involve acquaintance rape, inappropriate sexual contact, cheating on one's significant other, or any of a variety of other scenarios. No matter what the situation, invariably the following statement comes out: "I probably had too much to drink."

Psychologists, however, will not accept the simplistic explanation that risky sexual behavior is an inevitable consequence of excessive drinking. First of all, many people have poor impulse control; this trait can lead them to both drink and engage in risky behavior. For these people, therefore, drinking may not be the cause of the risky behavior.

Certain environmental circumstances—such as living in a fraternity house, being single, having parents who are often away from home—can encourage both drinking and risky behavior. Again, drinking may not be the cause of the

risky behavior. Also complicating the picture are studies showing that drinking in college students often occurs to enhance the pleasure of sex, or to make sex easier. In other words, the desire to have sex may be the cause of drinking, and not the other way around.

Research has also shown that if participants believe they have consumed alcohol in a placebo drink that tastes like alcohol but is not, they behave like people who actually have consumed alcohol. Expectations about the effects of alcohol, therefore, can play a major role in human behavior.

Research also shows that the effects of alcohol interact with the personality of the consumer and with the consumer's evaluation of the situation itself. Thus, if a man on a first date is drinking and determines that the costs of having sex is low relative to the benefits, then the likelihood of sex on that first date is increased by alcohol consumption. If, on the other hand, the dangers of risky sex with a new partner are clearly obvious in a situation, men who are drinking become more cautious about having risky sex. Thus, the relationship between alcohol and risky sex is complex. However, studies at least show that signals in situations can be structured in such a way to decrease the chance of risky behavior being elicited by consumption of alcohol.

We believe one aspect of this discussion should be stressed: Alcohol consumption should never be accepted as an excuse for engaging in risky behavior. Don't you just love it when some celebrity, politician, or other high-profile individual gets caught doing something wrong and quickly checks into a rehab facility? The message being conveyed is quite clear, but also disgusting: ''I did it, but it's not my fault. It was the demon rum. I have a disease. But look, I'm taking steps to correct the situation, so don't hold my behavior against me." Sorry, bozo. The booze didn't make you do it; you made you do it!

Our research question in this section deals with risky sexual behavior and drinking. Let's pose another question. How about general aggressive behavior? What does alcohol do to us? A lot of us know someone who seems very mild-mannered, calm, and even-tempered when sober; after a few drinks, however, this person becomes like a chain saw, angrily cutting through anyone who happens to be in the way.

"Did you hear that Joe punched someone in the mouth at the party the other night?"

"Yeh, I did. He must have been drunk, because he never would do anything like that sober."

QUESTION: *Will alcohol intoxication automatically make someone more aggressive?*
RESEARCH ANSWER: *No.*

ANALYSIS

No doubt you saw that answer coming, given our answer to the first question in this section. And, no doubt, you may raise strong objections to the answer. Like we said before, all of us have seen alcohol transform people in negative ways. In fact, you can find lots of evidence showing a firm relationship between aggressive behavior and alcohol consumption. Peter Giancola and Michelle Corman of the University of Kentucky note that alcohol is involved in about half of all violent crimes; intoxication has a huge effect on aggressive behavior. How, therefore, can we give a "no" answer to our question? Well, we cheated a bit in the way we phrased the question; we put in that word "automatic." Let's face it, when it comes to behavior, not many things are automatic. If behavior were that simple, there would be no need for psychology.

Giancola and Corman describe a couple of studies from their lab that illustrate how alcohol consumption is not necessarily going to increase aggressive tendencies. Their participants were men between 21 and 33 years of age. The men participated in a contest against another person (who was actually working with the experimenters) to see who could lift their finger off the space bar of a keyboard the fastest. Obviously, the participants could not be certain about the outcome, so the experimenters could predetermine who would win each trial.

The winners of the contest got to deliver electric shocks to the fingers of the other players, at either a "low," "medium," or "high" voltage level. On some trials, therefore, the participants received shocks of varying intensities, which they thought were coming from their opponents; on other trials, the participants were free to choose a shock level to deliver to their opponents. The shock intensity chosen by the participants after being told they had won a trial was considered a measure of aggression. That is, choosing to deliver a high-voltage level was considered a high-aggression response; choosing a low level was considered a low-aggression response.

During the reaction time contest, half of the participants also had to work on a distraction task. That is, while concentrating on raising their finger as quickly as possible from the space bar after a signal, half the men also had to concentrate on a computer screen in front of them and try to remember a sequence of events on the screen.

Half the men played the game after drinking a controlled amount of alcohol in orange juice. The other half drank only orange juice, although the rims of the glasses for both groups were sprayed with alcohol so they would think they were drinking alcohol in the orange juice. In fact, all participants were told that during the experiment they would consume the amount of alcohol found in three to four mixed drinks. The actual blood alcohol level in those receiving the alcohol averaged 0.1 percent, at or above the legal limit in most states.

The results showed that participants receiving alcohol delivered higher levels of shock to their opponent than did participants receiving the placebo, but only when they did not have the distraction task. Thus, alcohol increased aggression in those men who were concentrating on the task at hand, lifting their finger quickly, without any distracting task. On the other hand, for those participants who were engaged in the distraction task while also in the competitive task, quite different results were found; when the distraction task was added to the competition, alcohol groups actually tended to administer lower levels of shock to the opponent compared to the placebo groups. In this case, alcohol actually reduced aggression.

As the authors note, the results suggest that alcohol can either increase or decrease aggression; aggressive behavior is not an inevitable consequence of ingesting alcohol. Now, of course, we don't want to recommend boozing someone up as a way of calming their anger! We're sure you get the point, though. In fact, maybe this experiment just validates what many of us have known all along. What do we do when we're out with a friend who has had a little too much sauce and is beginning to become a little belligerent, nasty, and threatening to strangers who are around? We try to get our friend preoccupied with something or someone else. It might be tough to pull off at times, but basically and intuitively, we're providing our friend with a distraction to keep the alcohol from energizing aggressive tendencies.

Students often find themselves in conversations about alcohol, sex, and aggression. As we see in this section, the relationships are complex and provide another great example of the best answer to most psychological questions: "It depends!" Having some knowledge of these complexities can not only aid you in these informal discussions, but can also allow you to add to the sophistication of class discussion on these topics, as well as help you prepare more scholarly papers.

PRIMARY REFERENCES

Cooper, L. M. 2006. Does drinking promote risky sexual behavior? *Current Directions in Psychological Research* 15: 19–23.

Giancola, P. R. and M. D. Corman. 2007. Alcohol and aggression. *Psychological Science* 18: 649–55.

ADDITIONAL REFERENCES

Abbey, A. 2002. Alcohol-related sexual assault: A common problem among college students. *Journal of Studies on Alcohol, Suppl.* 14: 118–28.

Fals-Stewart, W. 2003. The occurrence of partner physical aggression on days of alcohol consumption: A longitudinal study. *Journal of Consulting and Clinical Psychology* 71: 41–52.

MacDonald, T. K., G. T. Fong, M. P. Zanna, and A. M. Martineau. 2000. Alcohol myopia and condom use: Can alcohol intoxication be associated with more prudent behavior? *Journal of Personality and Social Psychology* 78: 605–19.

Murphy, C., J. Winters, T. O'Farrell, W. Fals-Stewart, and M. Murphy. 2005. Alcohol consumption and intimate partner violence by alcoholic men: Comparing violent and nonviolent conflicts. *Psychology of Addictive Behaviors*, 19: 35–42.

8
Are Marijuana and Schizophrenia Related?

Although marijuana remains an illegal drug in America, its use has been decriminalized to the extent that many in our society see such use as a harmless recreational pastime. In fact, many people see "weed" as a much safer drug than alcohol, both medically and psychologically. That perspective, of course, comes primarily from marijuana users and is used to justify their drug use. The fact is, however, we have yet to see the medical establishment put out a statement that marijuana, when used moderately on a daily basis, can truly have beneficial health effects. On the other hand, such statements have been issued for alcohol.

We're not interested in joining the marijuana versus alcohol debate, although it is a good research question for students. Debating the problem in this book, however, would take us far from research results, which are our primary emphasis. We decided, therefore, to cast marijuana into a different type of question, one aimed directly at psychological functioning:

QUESTION: *Does marijuana use increase the risk of becoming schizophrenic?*
RESEARCH ANSWER: *Yes.*

ANALYSIS

First of all, let's make sure we know what schizophrenia is. This mental illness results from faulty brain functioning; things in the brain go haywire in a cognitive sense, and victims have difficulty maintaining contact with reality. They may see or hear things that are not really present; they may develop elaborate delusional beliefs and greatly distort the meaning of what people say and do to them; they may display totally inappropriate emotions in situations, or sometimes no emotion at all; they may think they are someone else, often famous or imagined (Elvis, perhaps, or a space alien), and have little sense of a unified self. In schizophrenia, the things that make us rational human beings—things like a coherent flow of thoughts, appropriate linking of thoughts and emotions, and a sense of self—are disrupted.

The reason for all this strange behavior and thinking is that the physical functioning of our brains is damaged. This damage can result from many causes, such as genetic propensities, disruptions in fetal development during pregnancy, extreme environmental trauma, or substances we consume. Our research question, of course, touches on this last possible cause. When we ingest marijuana and it enters our brain, do we run the risk of producing damage to the extent that schizophrenia could result?

In a huge study involving recruits in the Swedish Army, researchers assessed the drug habits of 50,000 men when they were 18 years old. These men were monitored over the next 15 years, with special attention given to whether they developed noticeable symptoms of schizophrenia as they got older. Remarkably, the marijuana users at age 18 were 600 percent more likely to be diagnosed with schizophrenia over the next 15 years than were nonusers. The heavier the use at 18, the more likely was the disorder to appear in subsequent years.

A variety of other findings generally support the conclusions from the Swedish study. For instance, 10 percent of those using marijuana in their early teens developed schizophrenic symptoms by age 18, compared to 3 percent of nonusers; the case histories of schizophrenics show that, compared to the nonschizophrenic control group, they are twice as likely to have used marijuana in their past; ⟨researchers estimate that around 10 percent of all cases of schizophrenia are linked to marijuana use during the teen years⟩Thus, the link is quite strong, and our young teens are really pointing a gun at their heads when they get stoned.

All you beer lovers, don't go getting pompous! Marijuana is not alone in leading the brain down the schizophrenic road. Joining the marching parade are alcohol, along with the usual suspects, LSD, methamphetamine, and other hallucinogenic substances. Those parents who are relieved to find their intoxicated son, "Just drank too many beers; thank God he doesn't do pot," should not be so relieved.⟨Excessive alcohol consumption during the teen years is putting the brain at severe risk for later problems in processing information and staying in contact with reality.⟩

What we should really find remarkable from all these findings is the casual manner in which so many parents readily have their children take psychotropic prescription drugs (antidepressants, antianxiety agents, and antipsychotic compounds) for what are often common symptoms of growing up and self-discovery. Ask your friends, "If weed, LSD, crystal meth, and bourbon can screw up our brains, why can't stuff like Haldol, Strattera, Wellbutrin, Zoloft, Paxil, Xanax, Buspar, and Zyprexa do the same thing?"

PRIMARY REFERENCE

Zammit, S., P. Allebeck, S. Andreasson, I. Lundberg, and G. Lewis. 2002. Self-reported cannabis use as a risk factor for schizophrenia: Further analysis of the 1969 Swedish conscript cohort. *British Medical Journal* 325: 1199–201.

ADDITIONAL REFERENCES

Bersani, G., V. Orlandi, D. Kotzalidis, and P. Pancheri. 2002. Cannabis and schizophrenia: Impact on onset, course, psychopathology and outcomes. *European Archives of Psychiatry and Clinical Neuroscience* 252: 86–92.

Brunette, M. F., K. T. Mueser, H. Xie, and R. E. Drake. 1997. Relationships between symptoms of schizophrenia and substance abuse. *Journal of Nervous Mental Disorders* 185: 13–20.

Cantor-Graae, E., L. G. Nordstrom, and T. F. McNeil. 2001. Substance abuse in schizophrenia: A review of the literature and a study of correlates in Sweden. *Schizophrenia Research* 48: 69–82.

Caspari, D. 1999. Cannabis and schizophrenia: Results of a follow-up study. *European Archives of Psychiatry and Clinical Neuroscience* 249: 45–49.

McDonald, C., and R. M. Murray. 2000. Early and late environmental risk factors for schizophrenia. *Brain Research Review* 31: 130–37.

PART TWO

RAISING THE LITTLE ONES

9
Does Stress during Pregnancy Harm the Fetus?

Expectant mothers are told to take care of themselves. They should not smoke or drink or use drugs; they need to eat well and take their vitamins; as much as possible they should keep up their exercise routines and maintain their weight gain within certain limits. What we don't hear as much is advice to mothers-to-be about staying calm, relaxed, and keeping stress at work and home to a minimum. Should this advice be more forthcoming?

Evidence relating maternal stress to development problems in offspring is fairly substantial in animal studies. For instance, studies have found that in rodents, offspring of stressed mothers show learning deficits, inability to handle stressful situations, and noticeable changes in brain structure. In monkeys, maternal stress has been linked in offspring to learning problems, reduced attention, and difficulties in social interactions with peers.

QUESTION: *Does maternal stress influence cognitive and emotional development of the child after birth?*

RESEARCH ANSWER: *We don't know.* Cop out! Cop out! What's with this "We don't know" answer? What happened to our pledge to deliver straightforward answers to questions posed in this book? Please bear with us as we provide our analysis.

ANALYSIS

First of all, let's note that in animal studies, we can systematically submit pregnant mothers to stress in ways that would be quite unacceptable and unethical at the human level. (Many would say that the animal studies are unethical, too, but that is an emotional issue beyond the scope of this book.) Animals can, for instance, be subjected to unpredictable and periodic noise, or uncomfortable confinement, or regular introduction to new and strange environments. No pregnant woman, however, is going to let researchers do such things to her, nor are ethical review boards at colleges and universities going to approve such studies. Thus, we are quite limited in how we can even begin to answer our question at the human level.

Basically, with human expectant mothers, we are left trying to assess how much stress a mom may or may not have had during her pregnancy, and then see if there's any relationship between that stress and the development of her child after birth. There are many problems with this type of methodology, of course, because we cannot control the intensity or nature of the stress during pregnancy. For instance, is living in Manhattan as a pregnant woman on 9/11 equivalent to undergoing a divorce or death of a loved one? Also, when we simply ask women about stress when they were pregnant, we have no control over when the stress occurred. By the same token, we must rely on subjective reports and memory, and these reports will be influenced by the fact that individuals perceive and appraise stress in quite different ways. Furthermore, our memories are far from accurate photographs of what we experienced in the past.

What we're saying, of course, is that the scientific rigor of research with humans on this topic is not quite what we want it to be, or what it is with animals. That is why we answered "We don't know" to our research question. Can we,

however, tilt in one direction or another? Is there any evidence suggesting that maternal stress has some harmful effects when it comes to development of the human child? Yes, there is, although the evidence is quite limited.

In one study, independent observers rated the ability of 8-month-old infants to pay attention. The results showed that attentiveness decreased as their mothers reported more stress during pregnancy. Another study reported a positive relationship between the amount of anxiety mothers reported they had during their pregnancy and the degree of similar negative emotions and behavior problems of their children when in preschool.

Some data, therefore, suggest a link between maternal stress and later functioning of the child. The evidence, however, does not allow us to make a confident, definitive statement that the link is there and that expectant mothers should be advised to seek environments and activities relatively free of stress. In fact, we believe that stress is never something we should seek to avoid, but is something we should learn to use to our advantage. The same rule probably applies to pregnant women. In fact, there is some evidence that moderate stress at appropriate times during pregnancy is beneficial to the fetus. Considering those complexities is best left for those students who choose to do additional research on this topic.

PRIMARY REFERENCE

DiPietro, J. A. 2004. The role of prenatal maternal stress in child development. *Current Directions in Psychological Science* 13: 71–74.

ADDITIONAL REFERENCES

Huizink, A., P. Robles de Medina, E. Mulder, G. Visser, and J. Buitelaar. 2002. Psychological measures of prenatal stress as predictors of infant temperament. *Journal of the American Academy of Child and Adolescent Psychiatry* 41: 1078–85.

Kofman, O. 2002. The role of prenatal stress in the etiology of developmental behavioral disorders. *Neuroscience and Biobehavioral Reviews* 26: 457–70.

Martin, R., J. Noyes, J. Wisenbaker, and M. Huttunen. 2000. Prediction of early childhood negative emotionality and inhibition from maternal distress during pregnancy. *Merrill-Palmer Quarterly* 45: 370–91.

Mulder, E., P. G. Robles de Medina, A. C. Huizink, B. R. Van den Bergh, J. K. Buitelaar, and G. H. Visser. 2002. Prenatal maternal stress: Effects on pregnancy and the (unborn) child. *Early Human Development* 70: 3–14.

O'Connor, T., J. Heron, J. Golding, M. Beveridge, and V. Glover. 2002. Maternal antenatal anxiety and children's behavioural/emotional problems at 4 years. *British Journal of Psychiatry* 180: 502–8.

10
Should Infants Sleep on Their Backs?

Sudden Infant Death Syndrome (SIDS) is a tragic event that raises questions and guilt in a parent's mind: "Did I do enough? Did I love my child enough? Am I a bad parent?" SIDS is certainly among the most tragic deaths because it occurs in the first year of life (mostly between 2 and 5 months of age), striking an apparently normal and healthy infant. Death usually occurs when everyone, including the victim, is sleeping. Consequently, parents can't look back at efforts they took to avert a tragedy, but can only wonder if their presence could have averted it.

QUESTION: *Is it best to have infants sleep on their backs?*
RESEARCH ANSWER: *Yes.*

ANALYSIS

There have been numerous medical explanations of "crib death" over the years. These explanations include some form of pneumonia, suffocation by vomit or bedding, air pollution, parental smoking, chemical composition of bedding or clothing, and parental neglect or abuse. None of these and other explanations, however, seems to fit the syndrome in any systematic fashion, and SIDS remains, for the most part, somewhat mysterious. Presently, medical professionals believe SIDS is not caused by external suffocation, choking, vomiting, poor parenting, or viral/bacterial infection.

In 1992, the American Academy of Pediatrics recommended that babies be placed on their backs for sleeping. Prior to that recommendation, about 2 babies of every 1,000 under the age of 1 died from SIDS. By the year 2000, SIDS cases in the USA had dropped about 50 percent. This marked decrease certainly suggested that whatever the cause of SIDS, some sort of breathing factor was involved.

Lewis Lipsitt of Brown University has presented an explanation that seems consistent with much of the data. He believes infants have an inborn reflex that produces head movement upwards and sideways whenever breathing is interrupted, such as when the infant might be lying on its stomach face down. After about 2 months of age, however, this protective reflex weakens and puts an infant in the stomach-down position at a higher risk for breathing blockage. With the weakened reflexive response, the baby now must rely on developed muscles that have been strengthened through activity since birth. If these muscles are somewhat weak, however, and the infant has a tendency toward quiet and calm behavior, movements required to move the head when in a stomach-down position may be quite difficult. The on-back sleeping position, of course, avoids this problem.

Lipsitt says that caretakers should not only place babies on their back for sleeping, but they should also encourage babies to "exercise" when awake and on their backs. Especially passive babies can be encouraged to move their arms and legs and head to strengthen muscles and develop generally defensive reactions. In other words, learning to ward off danger using behavioral measures can never begin too early. Even in premature babies, stimulation of muscles through touching, massage, and moving infants' limbs has been shown to have a beneficial effect. Preemies given such massage experience for 15 minutes about three times a day gain significantly more weight than untreated preemies, and they are released from the hospital more quickly than the untreated group.

We've all heard how great exercise is for adult health. It looks like we can extend those benefits of exercise downward in age and include our infants as well! And remember, when we touch, massage, and exercise our infants through movement of their limbs, we are showering them with attention and warmth; we are saying to them that we care, we love them, and we are there for them. That love and support, by the way, should not be expressed by sleeping with your infant! Doing so increases the odds of suffocation either from excessive bedding or from a sleeping adult rolling on top of the helpless infant.

PRIMARY REFERENCE

Lipsitt, L. P. 2003. Crib death: A biobehavioral phenomenon? *Current Directions in Psychological Science* 12: 164–70.

ADDITIONAL REFERENCES

Hunt, C. E. 2001. Sudden infant death syndrome and other causes of infant mortality: Diagnosis, mechanisms, and risk for recurrence of siblings. *American Journal of Respiratory and Critical Care in Medicine* 164: 346–57.

Lijowska, A. S., N. W. Reed, B. A. Merins Chiondi, and B. T. Thach. 1997. Sequential arousal and airway-defensive behavior of infants in asphyxial sleep environments, *Journal of Applied Physiology* 83: 219–28.

Naeye, R. 1980. Sudden infant death. *Scientific American* 242: 52–56.

Schluter, P. J., J. Paterson, and T. Percival. 2007. Infant care practices associated with sudden infant death syndrome: Findings from the Pacific Islands Family Study. *Journal of Pediatric Child Health* 43: 388–93.

Scragg, R.K.R., E. A. Mitchell, B. J. Taylor, A. W. Stewart, R. P. Ford, J. M. Thompson, E. M. Allen, and D. M. Becroft. 1993. Bed sharing, smoking, and alcohol in the sudden infant death syndrome. *British Medical Journal* 307: 1312–18.

Task Force on Infant Sleep Position and Sudden Infant Death. 2000. Report at year 2000. *Pediatrics: American Academy of Pediatrics* 195: 650–56.

11

Will Spanking Children Have Long-term Consequences?

It's happened to most of us. We're strolling somewhere in public, maybe in the mall or on a downtown sidewalk, and we come upon a mom obviously at the end of her rope. There she is beating the hell out of some snotty 2-year-old who has obviously been giving her trouble all day.

"I told you to stop pulling down your pants! (WHACK!) Do it one more time and I'll really let you have it! (WHACK!)"

Those "whacks" are well-placed smacks on the kid's behind, enough to cause the kid some pain and begin crying. We, of course, walk by with our noses in the air, muttering "Tsk, Tsk," and thinking, "Geez, lady, what's your problem? Can't you control your kid without such physical abuse? Don't you know that spanking is bad?" Ah, what's more self-assuring than smug arrogance?

When we ask our students if they plan on using spanking to discipline their children, most say they do not; they contend they will rely on other types of discipline, such as verbal reasoning, timeout, and taking away privileges before they will resort to actually hitting the child. (Interestingly, it is generally the male students who say they will have no hesitation to use spanking to discipline their children. In the words of one eloquent guy: "Hey, the only reason I behaved myself was because I knew my old man would beat the hell out of me if I didn't! It worked for me and it will work for my kids, too!")

Those students who say they will not spank are also those students who predict that having children and raising them will be the happiest and most satisfying time of their life (even better than the fun times of college, if that's possible!). That statement is interesting because research often shows that while engaged in the day-to-day activities of raising young children, parents actually rate childrearing activities as pretty low on the totem pole of satisfaction. Dinner and a movie with spouse or friends? A happy time. Fishing, golfing, the bridge club, volunteer activities with adults? Great times! Feeding the kids, running the birthday party, shopping for school clothes, watching the little league game, waiting at the school bus stop, etc., etc., etc.? Such things do not make the top ten of happy activities! There is indeed truth to the old adage that life begins when the dog dies and the kids leave home. Empty-nesters smile a lot.

Recently, one of our former students paid a visit with her husband and 4-month-old twins. They had been married for eight years before having children. Mom said, "We wanted to make sure we had lots of good times together we could always look back on. We know now we're tied up for 18 years with the kids; there won't be much time for just the two of us anymore."

She's right! She and her husband are in for some trying times, and they know it. Still, the fascinating thing about childrearing is that when the basic process is done and the kids leave home to make their way in the world, we parents often reflect that our children gave us the best and happiest times of our lives. The fact of the matter is that childrearing can be boring and stressful, but when it's all over and done, we view it as rewarding. When we reflect on hard times from a current perspective of comfort and satisfaction, the hard times do not seem so hard after all.

Even though many parents find childrearing quite a chore while the kids are young and at home, they try not to take out their frustrations on their children, especially by physically punishing them. Sometimes in the heat of battle, however, a well-placed smack on the buttocks or hand occurs almost automatically, before the parent even has time to reflect on the wisdom of the action. As a result, the parent may feel guilty afterward; "I spanked my kid. I'm a terrible parent and I'm ruining my kid for life!" Those sorts of feelings bring us to our question at hand:

QUESTION: *Is it psychologically OK to spank my child?*
RESEARCH ANSWER: *Yes.*

ANALYSIS

OK, we'll catch hell from someone for that answer ("You bums think it's OK to strike a child!!?"), but let's dig into this issue a bit. Let's note, by the way, that we're putting this question in the context of a child who is somewhere between 2 and 12. Physical punishment outside of that range is quite inappropriate (and even dangerous if the kid is bigger than you are!).

What does psychology have to say about spanking a child? First of all, we need to differentiate between (a) a well-placed hand on a clothed child's buttocks to make a firm point about an action (maybe something potentially dangerous), and (b) a consistent, daily pattern of hitting a child as the typical way of delivering discipline. The former is not going to damage a child for life, and we believe such occasional punishment can be used effectively to make important points to a child; the latter, however, the ongoing consistent pattern of physical punishment, just may do considerable psychological damage to a child. It is also important to distinguish spanking from out-and-out physical abuse, which would involve bruising and other physical injuries, and using objects like paddles and belts. We can't imagine any situation that condones such abuse.

Some basic research findings include the following (remember—any negative effects increase with the severity of the spanking):

- Spanking generally works in the sense that it produces compliance from the child. Most kids are not masochists. If they fear getting spanked and the punisher is around, they will not perform the forbidden action.

- Mild and occasional spanking is often positive and productive, reducing fighting and other potentially harmful behavior. Many researchers would add, however, that even mild spanking should be used only after other nonpainful punishment techniques like timeout, reasoning, or mild punishment have been tried extensively.

- Mild and occasional spanking can escalate. Nothing breeds aggressive behavior like aggressive behavior because aggression generally works in the short term. Guilt over an action tends to recede as the action is repeated again and again, making it easier to increase the intensity of the action.

- Spanking risks damaging the quality of your relationship with your child.

- Spanking presents an aggressive role model for the child and suggests aggression is an effective method of conflict resolution.

The potential negative risks of spanking, especially long-term, probably outweigh the positive, short-term benefits. All things being equal, it is probably best to try and find nonphysical ways to discipline a child. We are, however, only human. Those who find themselves losing control at a particular point in time, and impulsively delivering a firm spank to the child's posterior, should not be plunged into guilt or lose sleep over it. In addition, an important message may be getting through to the child. ("Whoa! Dad really doesn't want me to force little sis's tongue into the electric outlet!") Parents may, however, want to examine their reactions to the situation and try to prepare for other responses in the future.

One thing we'll say for certain: *A parent who physically punishes a child on a regular basis is probably insecure, on some sort of power trip, and has pretty weak interpersonal skills.* Parents can be powerful and effective without having to resort to physically hurtful actions. Unfortunately, parents who rely on punitive methods the most tend to be the least apt to use positive methods like approval and rewards. The reverse is also true.

PRIMARY REFERENCE

Kazdin, A. E., and C. Benjet. 2003. Spanking children: Evidence and issues. *Current Directions in Psychological Science* 12: 99–103.

ADDITIONAL REFERENCES

Baumrind, D., R. E. Larzelere, and P. A. Cowan. 2002. Ordinary physical punishment: Is it harmful? Comment on Gershoff 2002. *Psychological Bulletin* 128: 580–89.

Benjet, C., and A. E. Kazdin. 2003. Spanking children: The controversies, findings, and new directions. *Clinical Psychology Review* 23: 197–224.

Gershoff, E. T. 2002. Parental corporal punishment and associated child behaviors and experiences: A meta-analytic and theoretical review. *Psychological Bulletin* 128: 539–79.

Larzelere, R. E. 2000. Child outcomes of nonabusive and customary physical punishment by parents: An updated literature review. *Clinical Child and Family Psychology Review* 3: 199–221.

12
Will the 3-Year-Old Terror Be an Adult Terror?

You know the scene: Maybe you're visiting a friend or you have an older sibling with a child. You walk into the family room and there is a 3-year-old dismembering her older brother's GI-Joe doll. Arms and legs have been pulled from the sockets. The torso has been twisted into some grotesque shape, and the head has been smashed flatter than a pancake. A bayonet has been plunged into the chest. You survey the carnage with concern. "Do I see a budding serial killer here? Or maybe an aggressive man hater who will always lash out verbally and maybe even physically whenever a guy crosses her?" You mention your concern to your friend or your sister to come and check out the murderous scene, and what is the reaction? "Don't worry, she'll outgrow it."

Outgrow it. How many parents and grandparents have reassured each other that undesirable behavior, or disturbing interests displayed by a child, or even being overweight, will eventually enter the "outgrow it" void? "Don't worry," we tell ourselves and others, "this is only temporary. It's a stage and it won't last."

Maybe we're right; maybe what we're worried about will slowly recede, just like the habitual "No!" reply of the 2-year-old, or the incessant "Why?" reply of the 4-year-old. Then again, however, we always wonder if what we're seeing in very young children is predictive of what they will be like as adults. Let's put this concern into our next research issue:

QUESTION: *Can adult personality be predicted as early as 3 years of age?*
RESEARCH ANSWER: *Yes.*

ANALYSIS

In the research and theory world of psychology, this topic remains quite controversial. A lot of psychologists believe it makes sense that there would be continuity to development, that the basic seeds of personality are planted very early in life. According to this view, all of us interpret future experiences within a basic

core foundation of personality that has already been laid down when we were children. Other psychologists say such a view is a gross oversimplification and overlooks the strong effect our current environment can have on us. Thus, an angry, hostile, aggressive, and temperamental 8-year-old can, with the proper education, training, care, and nurturance, be transformed into a more productive and cooperative individual. This view, of course, gives us a lot of hope and optimism when it comes to dealing with children who have been abused and neglected early in their lives, and have developed a sour and angry view of the world. We believe we can turn them around in a very fundamental way.

On the other hand, what about the child who has been raised in a Brady Bunch environment? Can the kid who has been raised in a solid family, and who is described as kind and gentle, get in the wrong crowd and have that positive personality turned around into something darker and meaner?

To help answer some of these questions, Aushalom Caspi of the Institute of Psychiatry at King's College London, and the University of Wisconsin–Madison, studied more than 1,000 New Zealand children of varying income levels from age 3 to 26. Special emphasis was put on measuring their personality characteristics at various ages, roughly every two years. Beginning at age 3, each child was observed for 90 minutes by an investigator who had no prior knowledge about or contact with any of the children. The investigator rated each child on five personality categories: well-adjusted, undercontrolled, confident, inhibited, and reserved. Every two years for the next 23 years, each child was rated again on these dimensions. The new interviewers, of course, had no knowledge how a child had been rated previously.

At 26 years of age, participants filled out numerous personality questionnaires, and also had a friend, partner, or family member who knew them well complete a personality assessment of them. The results were clear in showing considerable personality consistency over time. Children characterized as undercontrolled, irritable, and impulsive at age 3 were found to be intolerant, easily upset, overreactive, and feeling mistreated and betrayed by others at age 26. Those described as inhibited, shy, and fearful at 3 were described as overcontrolled and nonassertive at 26. Confident, energetic, and outgoing 3-year-olds were nonconventional and extraverted at 26. Reserved and apprehensive 3-year-olds were unassertive, introverted, and shy at 26. Finally, well-adjusted 3-year-olds were also evaluated that way at 26.

We can certainly interpret these results to mean that it's quite dangerous to assume that children will "outgrow" particular personality traits they may show at a very early age. In fact, if those traits are somewhat undesirable, we should assume just the opposite and assume they will not outgrow them. Imagine a co-worker bringing a child into work for "bring a son/daughter to work day." Imagine further that the kid is a royal pain, rambunctious, impolite, loud, overactive, getting into everything, and disrupting the whole office. If the parent reassures co-workers that "Kids will be kids," or "I can't wait for him/her to grow out of this stage," we can only hope that someone will pull that parent aside and read the riot act. "This is no stage! You have a damn monster personality on your hands and you better start acting like a parent and help the kid channel some of these tendencies!"

There's a key phrase in that sentence: "Channel some of these tendencies." Just because we're saying that basic personality traits of adulthood may be strongly displayed in the very young child, we're not saying there's nothing a parent can do to help guide the child to use these traits in socially acceptable and productive ways. For instance, suppose a child literally pops out of the womb and shows him- or herself to be a very aggressive, outgoing, overbearing, domineering type who usually turns others off by this domineering, controlling behavior. Parents can help guide this child into channeling these aggressive traits into (a) determination to work hard with others, (b) initiative to plan and suggest courses of action in groups, and (c) leadership styles to help others cooperate and work toward a common goal.

As a psychology guru, you are now ready to offer some sound advice for your friends or add some words of wisdom to a paper on parenting. Parents can hope their kids are born with "good" personality traits, but their job is not to stand by helplessly if their kids are showing "bad" traits; the parents' job is not to try and stamp out those traits and demand their kids become something the kids are not. Their job is to guide their kids, to channel those basic personality traits into socially useful behaviors, and to help them become "who they are" by benefiting, not disrupting, society.

PRIMARY REFERENCE

Caspi, A., H. L. Harrington, B. Milne, J. W. Amell, R. F. Theodore, and T. E. Moffitt. 2003. Children's behavioral styles at age 3 are linked to their adult personality traits at age 26. *Journal of Personality* 71: 4.

ADDITIONAL REFERENCES

Bruer, J. T. 1999. *The Myth of the First Three Years*. New York: Free Press.

Caspi, A. 2000. The child is father of the man: Personality continuities from childhood to adulthood. *Journal of Personality and Social Psychology* 78: 158–72.

Hamer, D. 1997. The search for personality genes: Adventures of a molecular biologist. *Current Directions in Psychological Science* 6: 111–14.

McCrae, R. R., and P. T. Costa, Jr. 1997. Personality trait structure as a human universal. *American Psychologist* 52: 509–16.

McCrae, R. R., P. T. Costa, Jr., F. Ostendorf, A. Angleitner, M. Hrebíčková, M. D. Avia, J. Sanz, M. L. Sánchez-Bernardos, M. E. Kusdil, R. S. Woodfield, P. R. Saunders, and P. B. Smith. 2000. Nature over nurture: Temperament, personality, and life span development. *Journal of Personality and Social Psychology* 78: 173–86.

Roberts, B. W., and W. Friend-DelVecchio. 2000. Consistency of personality traits from childhood to old age: A quantitative review of longitudinal studies. *Psychological Bulletin* 126: 3–25.

13
Can Communities Encourage Children to Exercise?

American kids are getting fatter and fatter. We all know the culprits here: high-fat snack foods, video games, TV, the Internet, e-mail and chat rooms, cell phones, and, sometimes, lack of adult guidance and meager recreation facilities. Parents, of course, fight these evils all the time. Sometimes they are aided by organized activities like athletic leagues in soccer, swimming, basketball, softball, and baseball (although there can be a downside here when 10-year-old kids are playing a soccer match at 10 P.M. on a school night). At other times, however, parents are left with the ineffective tactic of yelling at the kid to log off the Internet and get outside and play. And then there can be the problem in some neighborhoods where the kid justifiably says to the yelling parent, "Where am I supposed to go and play?"

QUESTION: *Can careful city and neighborhood planning help increase physical activity in children?*
RESEARCH ANSWER: *Yes.*

ANALYSIS

We admit this question is probably a "gimme" and pretty commonsensical, but let's look at an interesting study conducted in the Buffalo–Niagara Falls metropolitan area of northwestern New York State. Leonard Epstein and colleagues at the University of Buffalo recruited boys and girls between the ages of 8 and 15 for this study. Using recordings in a personal log from both family members and the children, and using a device attached to clothing that measured amount of physical activity, the researchers were able to obtain accurate measures of the children's activity levels. The researchers also assessed the neighborhood characteristics where each child resided, with attention concentrated on housing density, number of street intersections, and amount of recreational park areas easily accessible (within walking distance) to the child's residence.

Epstein and his colleagues developed an activity plan that they asked the participating families to follow. During one three-week phase, the plan called for increasing physical activity of children in the family, and during another three-week phase the plan called for decreasing physical activity of the children. The families could actually earn some money according to how well the children attained the standards specified in the plan.

The results showed that compared to older children, young children had more difficulty decreasing their physical activity when required by the plan. Also, compared to girls, boys had more difficulty decreasing their physical activity when required to do so. Finally, children who lived in areas with large neighborhood parks had more trouble decreasing their physical activity than did children who lived in areas with no such neighborhood park.

You're probably saying, "What's the big deal here? These results seem pretty obvious." Maybe so, but how often do we see the obvious put into practice? For instance, Epstein's findings show that cities and neighborhoods can have a significant impact on children's behavior by providing them with recreational areas. The parent yelling at the child to "get off that computer and get outside" will have much more impact when able to identify a specific activity in a specific place. There is no guarantee, of course, because some kids develop powerful, comfortable, and rewarding habits with the TV, computer, and cell phone. But we're talking about increasing our odds of getting the child out of the house, not certainty! (In your discussions about human behavior, always keep this idea in your arsenal: Nothing is certain or 100 percent when we talk about human behavior. The best we can do is increase the odds that we're correct by identifying relevant factors involved. Think of psychologists as behavioral weather forecasters! Think in terms of risks and probabilities.)

We might also highlight the fact that, in Epstein's study, younger children were less able to reduce their activity when required to do so by the plan. Granted, we might say that young kids just can't follow directions because they're too impulsive. We might also say, however, that just like kittens, puppies, lion cubs, and young chimps, human children have a need to play and be active. Such activity is probably essential for proper body and brain growth. Think about that possibility the next time you read about the frightening increase in the use of antianxiety, antidepressant, and antipsychotic drugs in children under the age of 12. We use these agents like cosmetics to cover up unwanted behaviors, just as we use makeup to cover a skin blemish. Who knows what we are doing to the neurological development of these children by tranquilizing these children and dulling their basic play tendencies?

Epstein's finding that the younger children were less able to reduce their activity when required also carries a lesson for parents. Just as it is easier to teach a younger child a foreign language than an older child, so it is easier to guide young children into productive and healthy habits. We must remember that a key to getting children on a healthy life path is to allow them to associate healthy behaviors, like playing outside in parks and playgrounds, with rewards and satisfaction. Epstein's study reminds us that our research answer is given more confidently when we're talking about young children compared to the older ones. The older ones are more likely to have developed strong associations of reward and satisfaction with sedentary activities in the home environment. Of course, even the older ones are not beyond help. It's really never too late to get them off their butts and outside!

PRIMARY REFERENCE

Epstein, L. H., S. Raja, S. S. Gold, R. A. Paluch, Y. Pak, and J. N. Roemmich. 2006. Reducing sedentary behavior: The relationship between park area and the physical activity of youth. *Psychological Science* 17: 654–59.

ADDITIONAL REFERENCES

Bedino-Rung, A. L., A. J. Mowen, and D. A. Cohen. 2005. The significance of parks to physical activity and public health: A conceptual model. *American Journal of Preventive Medicine* 28: 159–68.

Epstein, L. H., and J. N. Roemmich. 2001. Reducing sedentary behavior: Role in modifying physical activity. *Exercise and Sport Science Reviews* 29: 103–8.

Epstein, L. H., J. N. Roemmich, F. G. Saad, and E. A. Handley. 2005. The value of sedentary alternatives influences child physical activity choice. *International Journal of Behavioral Medicine* 11: 236–42.

Ewing. R. 2005. Can the physical environment determine physical activity levels? *Exercise and Sport Science Reviews* 33: 69–75.

Saelens, B. E., J. F. Sallis, and L. D. Frank. 2003. Environmental correlates of walking and cycling: Findings from the transportation, urban design, and planning literatures. *Annals of Behavioral Medicine* 25: 80–91.

Timperio, A., D. Crawford, A. Telford, and J. Salmon. 2004. Perceptions about the local neighborhood and walking and cycling among children. *Preventive Medicine* 38: 39–47.

14
Will Kids Raised by Gays Become Gay?

The times they are a-changing! When your authors were in high school, the typical American family was headed by a barefoot and pregnant mom in the kitchen and a dad at work. Life generally followed scenes depicted in old TV shows like *Leave it to Beaver* and *Happy Days*. This was the Richie Cunningham era. If a teen girl got in a "family" sort of way (that means pregnant, a word that could not even be mentioned on TV shows in the 1950s), she seemed to disappear from school for a year. Talk was she went to live with her aunt in Iowa to help care for her sick uncle. But this scenario didn't seem to happen too often. In 1960, 5 percent of American children were born to unmarried women. Oh, how the times are a-changing! In 2002, the percentage of unwed births was 33 percent for whites and 66 percent for blacks!

The two-parent married household seems to be a thing of the past. In 2004 only 68 percent of American children lived with married parents. On the positive side, that percentage has not decreased in the last 10 years. Maybe the decline of the two-parent household has stopped.

Whereas single-parent families have certainly increased over the past 50 years, we should not discount the psychological benefits of marriage. For instance, of children born to unmarried parents living together, 75 percent will see their parents split up before they are 16 years old; the corresponding percentage for children born to married parents is a much lower 33 percent. Studies have also found that children reared in traditional two-parent families are more likely to stay in school, resist teen pregnancy, hold a job, and score higher on tests of both physical and mental health.

But what if the two parents are gay or lesbian? This is an emotionally laden issue in American society, a fact illustrated in a "viewpoint" column in the December 18, 2006 issue of *Time*. The author, James Dobson, writes about Mary Cheney, daughter of the vice-president of the United States at the time, who "is pregnant with a child she intends to raise with her lesbian partner." The theme of Dobson's article is that such an arrangement is unfortunate because "more than 30 years of social-science evidence indicates that children do best on every measure of well-being when raised by their married mother and father." Dobson goes on to quote professionals on the importance of *fathers* in child development.

Dobson is founder and chairman of Focus on the Family, and his article, which advocates saving and maintaining the traditional American family, is obviously written in the context of this position. At a gut level, many of us would tend to

agree with Dobson's conclusion that "The traditional family ... is still the foundation on which the well-being of future generations depends."

Agreement with that statement, however, is irrelevant to our purpose here.
Our approach in this book is not one of advocacy. In fact, no matter what topic
we consider, we attempt to present some objective information independent of
any emotionally based attachment to a particular point of view. So with that goal
in mind, let's return to our basic question concerning the psychological stability
of children raised by gays. It's a straightforward question, and we will give you a
straightforward answer.

QUESTION: *Does being raised by gay or lesbian parents adversely affect the child's
development?*
RESEARCH ANSWER: *No.*

ANALYSIS

First of all, let's note that this area of research is relatively new. There is not what
we would call a voluminous literature on this topic. Second, let's note that the
available population to study is not exceedingly large. Even so, some statistical
institutes give estimates of adopted children in America living with gay or lesbian
couples that are as high as 65,000—more than 4 percent of all adoptees. Third,
we can note that some studies involve children who were born and raised for a
few years by heterosexual parents before living with same-sex partners, and some
involve children who were raised from birth by gay/lesbian couples. So, some
qualifications can be added to our research answer.

Qualifications aside, one would expect that over a research period of nearly
two decades, if there were any fundamental developmental dangers from being
raised by same-sex parents, some sort of trend would be apparent, but none has
been found. Parental sexual orientation has yet to be demonstrated as a relevant
variable in measures of child and adolescent emotional or cognitive development.
In fact, the quality of the parent-child relationship appears to be more strongly
linked with development than parental sexual orientation. Day-to-day interactions
between parent and child, and the strength of the supportive bond between parent and child, continue to emerge as the crucial factors in fostering healthy child
development.

This area, however, needs a lot of additional research. And like any behavioral
research area, subsequent studies will conclude, "Same-sex parents are not harmful *but*...." There are always "buts" in psychological research, and they are to be
expected. As for the gay/lesbian parent topic, however, our core conclusion is,
"Parental sexual orientation does not appear to have any profound effects on
child development."

One intriguing fact is that in 2007, 10 states had laws permitting gay/lesbian
couples to adopt children. We say *intriguing* because most of these states also ban
gays and lesbians from entering into a legal marriage. We can ask, "Where is the
logic in not allowing a couple to marry, but allowing them to adopt a child?"
The answer is actually pretty simple: Adoption laws are directed at improving the
welfare of the child, not at advocating gay rights. In fact, unmarried heterosexual
couples are also allowed to adopt children. Once again, the thinking is pretty
clear: As long as there is no clear and consistent evidence that adoption by
unmarried couples, whether gay or straight, is harmful to a child, the child is certainly better off in a two-parent household than in a one-parent household.

Supporters of laws permitting joint adoption by couples, therefore, say such laws are directed at the child's welfare. (Opponents like the Roman Catholic Church could not disagree more strongly, and say we cannot separate child welfare issues from issues of morality and the Judeo-Christian tradition of our society.)

Before leaving this topic, let's pose a different question, but one that many might see as relevant to the one we have just discussed:

QUESTION: *Are gay and lesbian relationships less stable than married heterosexual relationships?*
RESEARCH ANSWER: *Yes.*

ANALYSIS

We're going to define the word "stable" in our question as referring to the likelihood of ending the relationship. This particular definition is important because, let's face it, there are a lot of unstable marriages and relationships where, for some reason, the couple stays together and toughs it out.

Kurdek describes a study of 1,021 married heterosexual couples, 2,333 cohabiting heterosexuals, 493 gay cohabitors, and 335 lesbian cohabitors. After 18 months, the dissolution rate for each of these categories was 4 percent for married heterosexuals, 14 percent for cohabiting heterosexuals, 13 percent for gay cohabitors, and 18 percent for lesbian cohabitors. The most obvious conclusion here is that married heterosexuals are less likely to dissolve their relationship than cohabitors, whether heterosexual, gay, or lesbian. A similar finding was found in a survey of couples in Sweden in 1995. We might note that a gay or lesbian union in Sweden has legal status as a registered partnership. In spite of the legality, however, dissolution rates were 11 percent for lesbians and 14 percent for gays, compared to only 8 percent for heterosexuals.

The meaning of statistics like these, of course, is in the eye of the beholder. One may note that the dissolution rates are higher for gays and lesbians than for heterosexual married couples. One may counter, however, that in the United States numerous legal, moral, religious, and ethical forces work against dissolution of a marriage compared to barriers to dissolution of a gay/lesbian relationship. One may also note that in both surveys summarized above, the vast majority of relationships, whether heterosexual or homosexual, remained intact during the period of the surveys.

PRIMARY REFERENCES

Kurdek, L. A. 2005. What do we know about gay and lesbian couples? *Current Directions in Psychological Science* 14: 251–54.

Patterson, C. J. 2006. Children of lesbian and gay parents. *Current Directions in Psychological Science* 15: 241–44.

ADDITIONAL REFERENCES

Fulcher, M., E. L. Stufin, R. W. Chan, J. E. Scheib, and C. J. Patterson. 2005. Lesbian mothers and their children: Findings from the Contemporary Families Study. In *Recent Research on sexual Orientation, Mental Health, and Substance Abuse,* edited by A. Omoto and H. Kurtzman (281–99). Washington, DC: American Psychological Association.

Gartrell, N., A. Deck, C. Rodas, H. Peyser, and A. Banks. 2005. The National Lesbian Family Study: 4. Interviews with the 10-year-old children. *American Journal of Orthopsychiatry* 75: 518–24.

Kurdek, L. A. 2001. Differences between heterosexual-nonparent couples and gay, lesbian, and heterosexual-parent couples. *Journal of Family Issues* 22: 727–54.

Kurdek, L. A. 2003. Differences between gay and lesbian cohabiting couples. *Journal of Social Personal Relationships* 20: 411–36.

Kurdek, L. A. 2004. Are gay and lesbian cohabiting couples *really* different from heterosexual married couples? *Journal of Marriage and Family* 66: 880–900.

Wainright, J. L., and C. J. Patterson. 2006. Delinquency, victimization, and substance use among adolescents with female same-sex partners. *Journal of Family Psychology* 20: 526–30.

Wainright, J. L., S. T. Russell, and C. J. Patterson. 2004. Psychosocial adjustment and school outcomes of adolescents with same-sex parents. *Child Development* 75: 1886–98.

15
Is Daycare Psychologically Harmful to the Child?

Years ago, the typical early morning family scene in America involved the husband heading out for work, leaving the wife behind to get the kids off to school and prepare for a day of domestic duties. Today, however, it is much more common for both husband and wife not only to be involved parents, but also to have active careers. When the career involves leaving home daily for the workplace, child care becomes an important family issue.

Child psychology teaches us that early human development is greatly influenced by the quality of the early child-caregiver attachment. Most parents, especially those with a college education, are aware of this fact. Consequently, when they must leave their children and spend hours in the workplace, they worry whether having others care for their children will harm the quality of their bond with the children. In this section, we want to focus this concern specifically around a daycare center, where parents drop off their children and leave them with other children in the care of adult child care workers.

QUESTION: *Will daycare negatively affect my child's development?*
RESEARCH ANSWER: *No.*

ANALYSIS

A lot of the psychological research on daycare has focused on the parent-child relationship. That is, will having a child in daycare somehow weaken the bond between parent and child? We see this concern in movies and TV shows. You know the scene: Mom drops the child off at the daycare facility before heading off to work. The kid jumps into the arms of a worker and mom looks longingly, wondering if she's being replaced as the primary caregiver. Mom need not worry, however. The research shows it is the quality of her time with her son or daughter that matters, not necessarily the quantity of time.

We do not want to suggest there are no concerns we need to address when considering daycare for a child. It would appear, for instance, that the *quality* of daycare is very important in influencing early child development. Intellectual, verbal, and social competence skills increase in children who are in high-quality daycare settings. What are the important factors defining quality?

- The child:staff ratio. The smaller, the better.
- The number of children in the setting. The smaller, the better.

- Education and training level of the daycare staff.

- The materials (toys, books, etc.) available, and the degree to which the staff encourages their use in productive ways.

- The responsiveness, sensitivity, and warmth shown to the child by the staff. ⟨Children function best when there is an optimistic and positive emotional atmosphere in the center.⟩

The first four items in the above list are much easier to assess than the last one, but parents would be wise to try and assess the last one through surprise visits, observation, and recommendations from friends and acquaintances. Such assessment is worth doing because the last characteristic can compensate for a less-than-desirable score on one of the first four. For instance, especially warm, committed, and sensitive caregivers could cancel out the disadvantages of a somewhat less than ideal child:staff ratio.

One little gem concerning daycare is covered in the August 2004 issue of the journal, *Cancer Epidemiology, Biomarkers and Prevention* (see Marshall, 2004). This study found that children who attended daycare for at least one year prior to kindergarten were significantly less likely to develop Hodgkin's lymphoma as adults. One interpretation of this finding is that⟨daycare attendance exposes children to all sorts of infections and helps strengthen the immune system.⟩ Maybe so, but more such systematic observations and more direct measures of immune-system functioning are necessary before we add this dimension to the daycare topic.

Let's not forget one other important thing: Women who work outside of the home are often better off psychologically than women who don't. We should not take that statement as criticism of stay-at-home moms. Many such moms are perfectly happy, and some working moms are miserable. The problem is that the media seems to cast the working mom in a pressure-cooker environment and as someone who is just too tired at the end of the day to devote quality time to her children. There are some interesting research findings in this area. Compared to nonworking women, working women

- show lower cholesterol levels.

- have a lower incidence of general illness.

- are less depressed.

- say their jobs help serve as an outlet for the stresses of home and childrearing.

What these findings suggest is that working moms have no need to fear playing multiple roles in their life. Comfort level is the key. In fact, heading home on Friday for a weekend with the toddlers after a particularly tough week can be very pleasant and invigorating; by the same token, heading to work on Monday after a weekend of dealing with diapers, tantrums, and crying might be equally pleasant and invigorating!

PRIMARY REFERENCE

Marshall, N. L. 2004. The quality of early child care and children's development. *Current Directions in Psychological Science* 13: 165–68.

ADDITONAL REFERENCES

Ahnert, L., H. Rickert, and M. E. Lamb. 2000. Shared caregiving: Comparisons between home and child care settings. *Developmental Psychology* 36: 339–51.

Harms, T., R. M. Clifford, and D. Cryer. 1998. *Early Childhood Environment Rating Scale: Revised edition.* New York: Teachers College Press.

NICHD Early Child Care Research Network. 2002. Child-care structure–process–outcome: Direct and indirect effects of child-care quality on young children's development. *Psychological Science* 13: 199–206.

Peisner-Feinberg, E. S., M. R. Burchinal, and R. M. Clifford. 2001. The relation of preschool child-care quality to children's cognitive and social developmental trajectories through second grade. *Child Development* 72: 1534–53.

16
Can Anatomically Correct Dolls Help Children Describe Abuse?

When accusations of sexual abuse against children are made against an adult, we often turn to the children themselves to provide us with evidence. If a parent goes to the authorities or a health professional with suspicions of inappropriate behavior against a child, the child will often undergo an interview procedure by a professional. Sounds OK, until we realize that interviewing a child is a tricky proposition because the youngster can be very suggestible and vulnerable; even the way a question is worded can bias the child's response. A variety of studies have also shown that if interviewers believe the accusation is true, they tend to structure the interview in such a way that children's answers suggest that abuse occurred. Other problems that arise when interviewing a possible child victim include language and comprehension issues, embarrassment, and shame.

In an attempt to get around some of the problems when questioning children about possible sexual abuse, anatomically correct dolls might be used. The thinking here is that by allowing the child simply to point to areas of the doll's body, more accurate accounts of what actually happened to them will emerge.

QUESTION: *Do anatomically correct dolls increase accuracy in children's accounts of how they may have been touched.*
RESEARCH ANSWER: *No.*

ANALYSIS

Maggie Bruck and Stephen Ceci of McGill University in Montreal report an interesting study that allowed them to test the usefulness of anatomically correct dolls. In the study, 3- and 4-year-old children received a medical exam from a pediatrician with a parent and/or a nurse present. Some of the children received a routine genital examination as part of the procedure and some did not. After the exam, the children were questioned about it, and they were given an anatomically correct doll so they could show the interviewer precisely what the doctor had done to them. The kids were also allowed to use some standard medical tools (tongue depressor, stethoscope) to show how they were used in the exam.

Some of the children's depictions of how their exam proceeded were startling because they were so totally inaccurate. Children who had received a genital exam, and even some of those who had not, indicated that the doctor not only had touched their genital areas, but also had hit their genitals with an instrument, or inserted the instrument or a finger into one or several body orifices. None of these actions, of course, ever occurred. Imagine for a minute that this physician was on trial, and a videotape of the child explaining the examination using the doll was shown to the jury. Can you guess what the verdict would be? Some jurors would want to hang the doctor right there in the courtroom!

What's going on here? How could it be that the use of the doll could produce such blatant inaccuracies? If you think about the situation for a minute, the answer is not really all that complicated. First of all, both the instruments and the doll are new and fascinating. What do children do with such things? That's right—they play with them! What's happening is that this incredible doll, with its interesting moving parts and cavities, is eliciting play activities from the child. The props allow for all sorts of neat actions, and the child plays them out! Unfortunately, in doing so, any account of what actually happened during the exam is, to say the least, exaggerated and inaccurate.

If anyone ever mentions one of these dolls as a good way to increase accuracy when a child is trying to describe an event, send out a warning flag and say, "Whoa, there! Let me tell you how those dolls can be a real problem." Remind your listeners that when children suggest they have been touched inappropriately, our protective instincts are aroused. Furthermore, if the accused is on our hate list (an ex, for instance), the accusation gives us a chance to lash out. The fact is, however, calm heads are needed when children act out what someone "did to me."

PRIMARY REFERENCE

Bruck, M., and S. Ceci. 1997. The suggestibility of young children. *Current Directions in Psychological Science* 6: 75–78.

Bruck, M., S. Ceci, and E. Francoeur. 2000. Children's use of anatomically detailed dolls to report genital touching in a medical examination: Developmental and gender comparisons. *Journal of Experimental Psychology: Applied* 6: 74–83.

ADDITIONAL REFERENCES

Karlin, R. A., and M. T. Orne. 1996. Commentary on *Borawick v. Shay*: Hypnosis, social influence incestuous child abuse, and satanic ritual abuse: The iatrogenic creation of horrific memories for the remote past. *Cultic Studies Journal* 13: 42–95.

Lynn, S. J., and M. R. Nash. 1994. Truth in memory: Ramifications for psychotherapy and hypnotherapy. *American Journal of Clinical Hypnosis* 36: 194–208.

Scheflin, A. W., and D. Brown. 1996. Repressed memory or dissociative amnesia: What the science says. *Journal of Psychiatry and Law* 24: 143–88.

Sheehan, P. 1988. Confidence, memory, and hypnosis. In *Hypnosis and Memory*, edited by H. Pettinati (96–127). New York: Guilford Press.

Spanos, N. P., and J. McLean. Hypnotically created pseudomemories: Memory distortions or reporting biases? *British Journal of Experimental Clinical Hypnosis* 3: 155–59.

17
Do Material Rewards Ruin Children's Fun?

If we try and get our kids to do things by giving them some sort of material reward like money, a lollipop, a gold star, a trophy, or whatever, does that type of reward tend to stifle their interest in the task they are performing? Does the reward take the fun out of play and turn it into work?

A retired psychologist lived down the street from a middle school (grades 6, 7, and 8—the jungle years). One year, a group of three boys began to mess with his car, which was parked on the street in front of his house. He was, after all, an old

man, and what better fun than to pile leaves, sticks, rocks, and dirt on his car every morning. They weren't interested in damaging the vehicle, but just enjoyed showing their superiority by piling junk on the car.

Never mess with a psychologist! One day he came out of the house and yelled, "Good job, kids. Come here. I've got a dollar for each of you."

"Huh?" they wondered. "The old bird wants to pay us for messing up his car?"

For the next two weeks, the ritual repeated itself. The kids would come by every morning, toss whatever lawn debris was available onto the car, and then go and collect their dollar for a job well done. They figured the old man was nuts, but what the hell, they were getting a free soda every day (these were good wholesome kids!).

Then it happened. One day they trashed his car, but he didn't come out to give them the buck. They went to the front door and rang the bell. When he came to the door they asked, "Where's our dollar? We dumped grass and leaves and dirt all over your car like always. Where's our pay?"

"Times are tough for me, kids," he replied. "I've got to cut back on my spending so I can't pay you anymore. Sorry."

"Well screw you, buddy," one of them said. "You don't pay, then we're not piling dirt on your car anymore!"

OK, OK, maybe the story wouldn't end like that, but you get the point. When kids are having fun doing something (called intrinsic enjoyment) and we come along and begin to give them some material (extrinsic) reward for doing so, are we going to destroy their intrinsic enjoyment in doing the task?

QUESTION: *Will giving material rewards to children destroy their intrinsic fun in doing a task?*
RESEARCH ANSWER: *No.*

ANALYSIS

Several studies with young children show that giving them a prize for something they enjoy doing tends to make them lose interest in the task once the prize is withdrawn. In other words, the prize seems to turn play into work. As always, however, things are not that simple. When analyzing the effects of rewards on one's interest, we need to distinguish between rewarding for simply doing something versus rewarding someone for increasing their performance level of something they already do. When we are rewarded for doing something well, not just for doing it, then the reward will not decrease our intrinsic interest in the task.

We need not shy away from dispensing material rewards to our children for their behavior. Sports trophies, gold stars in the classroom, money for chores—all have an important place in teaching children about their world. Obviously, however, we must not overdo it. No coach should want youngsters to compete solely to obtain the league championship trophy; there is always an intrinsic enjoyment of, and respect for, the sport that must be conveyed by the coach. No matter what the activity, children should be taught about the two greatest imposters they will ever face: success and failure. Both experiences are imposters because one will have us believe we are better than we probably are; the other will have us believe we are worse than we probably are. An excessive emphasis on material rewards, of course, will magnify the importance of success, and overlook the importance of failure in teaching the athlete about persistence and hard work. Winning is not everything; it is the effort put forth to win that is everything.

One final point: Social praise is an effective supplement to material rewards. Praise from others can help maintain intrinsic interest in a task and even prove to be an effective substitute for material rewards. Bill, a colleague, told us how one day his 8-year-old daughter Anne received all A's on her report card. "You know," Anne told him, "Jen's parents give her $20 for every A she gets."

"Well," Bill replied, "I'm not Jen's dad. I can tell you, though, how proud your mother and I are of you. You do a great job at school; you study and work hard, and that shows us the kind of person you are. You know, mom and I were talking last night that this weekend would be nice to take a trip to the zoo or maybe even go swimming at the lake. [Anne likes both of these activities.] You've been working so hard at school lately, and done such a good job, why don't you choose the family outing this weekend."

The great part of the story is that Anne received a fantastic *intrinsic* reward for her performance (choosing a family activity), and Bill had $20 to put toward the zoo tickets that weekend.

PRIMARY REFERENCE

Cameron, J., K. M. Banko, and W. D. Pierce. 2001. Pervasive negative effects of rewards on intrinsic motivation: The myth continues. *Behavior Analyst* 24: 1–44.

ADDITIONAL REFERENCES

Cameron, J., and W. D. Pierce. 1994. Reinforcement, reward, and intrinsic motivation: A meta-analysis. *Review of Educational Research* 64: 363–423.

Deci, E. L., R. Koestner, and R. M. Ryan. 1999. A meta-analytic review of experiments examining the effects of extrinsic rewards on intrinsic motivation. *Psychological Bulletin* 125: 627–68.

Eisenberger, R., L. Rhoades, and J. Cameron. 1999. Does pay for performance increase or decrease self-determination and intrinsic motivation? *Journal Personality and Social Psychology* 77: 1026–40.

Lepper, M. R., M. Keavney, and M. Drake. 1996. Intrinsic motivation and extrinsic rewards: A commentary on Cameron and Pierce's meta-analysis. *Review of Educational Research* 66: 5–32.

18
Are Movie Portrayals of Smoking Harmful?

Check out a movie on the Turner Classic Movies TV station sometime. It is truly amazing how smoking is so prominent. Characters interact with one another and almost always have a cigarette in hand. Many of these movies, of course, were made in the 1930s, 1940s, and 1950s, decades when smoking was an acceptable part of the social scene. Whereas movies made toward the latter part of the twentieth century did not eliminate smoking behavior in characters, the behavior was certainly seen far less than in the earlier movies. Lately, however, it appears that smoking is making a comeback; it is not at all unusual to see characters smoke their way through the entire movie. In fact, smoking has also made its way into made-for-TV movies. The recent TNT production of *The Company* features a prominent character who chain-smokes his way through investigations.

Whether on the big screen or on TV, directors and camera operators love characters who smoke. The bending willows of smoke from a cigarette do wonders for conveying an atmosphere and catching surrounding light. Character development is also enhanced by smoking, a habit that often can add depth, intensity, and intrigue to a character. The problem, for many people, is that using smoking to augment artistic creativity is at odds with concerns about the health of our society. At a time when smoking has become a serious health concern, many worry that the depiction of smoking in the movies runs against health initiatives to reduce cigarette use in America, especially among young people. The argument goes something like, "How can we possibly reduce smoking in young folks when characters they admire and identify with in films are shown smoking?" What about it? Is there any evidence for this position? Does Hollywood encourage smoking when movies glamorize hero figures who smoke?

QUESTION: *Given certain conditions, does exposure to movies in which smoking occurs increase smoking in the viewer?*
RESEARCH ANSWER: *Yes.*

ANALYSIS

The affirmative answer to our question probably doesn't surprise you. There's a good bit of research in psychology that supports the association between smoking in movie characters and movie viewers. Read that question carefully, however, because there is a code phrase in there that is the key to your psychology prowess: "Given certain conditions." We can easily picture someone saying to you, "All this smoking in the movies is terrible. It sends a message to kids that smoking is cool." OK, fair enough. But the fact of the matter is, the association really depends on some other factors that need to be present. When you describe those factors, people around you will bow in awe and deference.

Sonya Dal Cin and her colleagues at the University of Waterloo in Ontario, Canada, report an experiment that identifies important factors responsible for the association between movies depicting smoking and viewer smoking. In the

study, college students first completed an extensive questionnaire about their attitudes toward smoking and whether they smoked. The questionnaire also assessed
the students' tendency to "get involved" in books, TV shows, and movies. As you
probably know, some people get so immersed in print and visual stories that they
are almost transported into the fantasy world. Others are more ho-hum about
such things.

Several weeks after completing the questionnaire the students watched one of
two 36-minute segments from the movie *Die Hard*. One group saw a segment that
involved Bruce Willis smoking heavily; the other group saw a 36-minute segment
in which Willis's character was not smoking. Following the film clip, students
completed another questionnaire. They answered items about the film, what they
thought of Willis's character portrayal, and how much they identified with his
character. The students then went to a nearby computer lab to participate in a
"second study." The researchers wanted to make sure the students did not associate this second phase with viewing the movie, so they made it seem totally separate from the movie evaluation.

In the second phase, the students completed a lengthy survey about smoking.
They indicated whether they smoked, how likely they would be to begin smoking
in the future, how they perceived people who smoked, and how much they associated various smoking-related items as consistent with their self-image.

The results showed that identification with the character portrayed in the
movie by Willis was a key factor. By *identification*, we mean the extent to which the
viewer admires the character's qualities and wants to be like the character. Specifically, if a nonsmoking viewer showed a strong identification with the Willis character, watching the smoking film clip made it more likely that the viewer would
indicate an intention to smoke in the future. That intention did not occur, however, in students who watched the nonsmoking film clip. This intention to smoke
in the future was also associated with a stronger link between smoking-related
items and self-image. Thus, nonsmokers who identified with the film character
were affected by the smoking behavior and made the smoking behavior
consistent with their own self-image.

Let's put these results into an appropriate context. The researchers are not
saying that we can take a random nonsmoker to the movies where there's a lot of
smoking going on among the main characters, and have our companion leave
the theatre asking, "Where can I buy some cigarettes?" Nothing is that simple.
The researchers are saying, however, that if we have a nonsmoker who tends to
get swept up in a movie story, and develops a strong identification with a main
character in the movie who smokes a lot in the film.... Well, then we have put in
motion a set of circumstances that makes the viewer's beliefs and attitudes toward
smoking more positive and normal in the viewer's eyes, and increases the likelihood that this viewer may try smoking in the future.

There are a lot of "ifs" in that last sentence, but that's what psychology is all
about. Research in psychology is really the search for "ifs." There are few abso-
lutes when it comes to behavior. The son of the alcoholic may become an alcoholic assuming some "ifs" are present. Let's search for those "ifs." Our search is
no different than asking, "When spelling a word in English, does 'i' come before
'e'?" Not if there's a "c" beforehand. And even when there's a "c," there are
some weird exceptions that seem quite foreign to the rule!

Your friends probably don't give a damn about "ifs," so don't mince words
when discussing this issue. "Let me tell you, I can show you evidence that says
when characters in a movie smoke, that movie contributes to a higher level of

smoking in society. Hollywood does no favors to the health condition of this country!''

One of your friends might respond, ''Bull! I don't smoke and I watch movies all the time where the characters smoke.''

''Yes,'' you reply, ''but you apparently do not strongly identify with those characters. You're able to distinguish the fictional character from the reality of your own life and self-concept.'' You are ''the man''! A master stroke! You have used your knowledge of an ''if'' to disarm your friend through flattery, and show your impressive knowledge at the same time.

PRIMARY REFERENCE

Dal Cin, S., B. Gibson, M. P. Zanna, R. Shumate, G. T. Fong. 2007. Smoking in movies, implicit associations of smoking with the self, and intentions to smoke. *Psychological Science* 18: 559–63.

ADDITIONAL REFERENCES

Dalton, M. A., J. D. Sargent, M.L. Beach, L. Titus-Ernstoff, J. J. Gibson, M. B. Ahrens, J. J. Tickle, and T. T. Heatherton. 2003. Effect of viewing smoking in movies on adolescent smoking initiation: A cohort Study. *Lancet* 362: 281–85.

Gibson, B. 2007. Cigarette smoking in the movies: The influence of product placement on attitudes toward smoking and smokers. *Journal of Applied Social Psychology* 30: 1457–73.

Hines, D., R. N. Saris, and L Throckmorton-Belzer. 2000. Cigarette smoking in popular films: Does it increase viewers' likelihood to smoke? *Journal of Applied Social Psychology* 30: 2246–69.

McTiernan, J. (Director). 1988. *Die Hard* [Motion picture]. United States: Twentieth Century Fox.

Pechmann, C., and C. F. Shih. 1999. Smoking scenes in movies and antismoking advertisements before movies: Effects on youth. *Journal of Marketing* 63: 1–13.

Tickle, J. J., J. G. Hull, J. D. Sargent, M. A. Dalton, and T. F. Heatherton. 2006. A structural equation model of social influences and exposure to media smoking on adolescent smoking. *Basic and Applied Social Psychology* 28: 117–29.

19
Can Playing Video Games Produce Antisocial Behavior?

For over 40 years, psychologists have studied the effects of TV violence on children's behavior. The general consensus of these studies should not surprise any of us: Yes, violent and aggressive behavior can be facilitated, even caused, by watching such behavior on TV. Of course, like everything else, it helps when particular factors are present, those pesky ''ifs'' we talked about in the previous section. In the case of TV, the likelihood that a child is influenced is increased if the child sees TV depictions as reflecting reality; if the child tends to identify with and admire an aggressive character; and if the child is being raised in a fairly cold, rejecting home with minimal parental supervision. In other words, it is fair to say that when talking about the potential influence of TV violence on a child, there are risk factors. The Brady Bunch kids are not likely to go out and terrorize the neighborhood after watching violent TV shows. Violent TV simply is not reinforced by the more dominant nonviolent influences in their primary environment.

Research attention is now turning to video games. The American Psychiatric Association even wants to have a new diagnostic category called video-game addiction. In case you have not noticed, some of these games are incredibly realistic and violent. Even the good guys (police officers) get blown away! We have often asked our college students about these games, because many play them. When asked, "Don't you think the explicit nature of the images and the violence encourages players to act out aggressive tendencies more readily?" they laugh at us.

"It's not real," they say. "It's harmless entertainment." We wonder if what they say is true for the 12-year-olds playing these things at the arcade in the mall!

QUESTION: *Does playing violent video games have negative effects on players?*
RESEARCH ANSWER: *Yes.*

ANALYSIS

OK, you're going to bring up the Brady Bunch example, and we agree. There are always risk factors to consider, even when we are looking at explicitly violent video games. Still, there's good solid evidence linking violent games to aggressive feelings and behaviors in kids. Sometimes, of course, the negative effects of a video game can be very subtle.

At Purdue University, Brad Sheese and William Graziano had undergraduates play a violent or nonviolent version of a video game. The major difference in the versions was that the violent one involved the use of weapons and killing opponents. After playing the game, all the players participated in a team exercise to earn money. The exercise allowed them either to cooperate and trust a partner, or to decide such cooperation was not worth the risk. The choices were structured in such a way that each one had costs and benefits, but cooperation could lead to mutual gain.

The results were clear. Those who played the violent video game were much less likely to choose to cooperate with a partner. They were more likely to choose the option that involved more exploitation of the partner.

When we read about studies looking at the effects of TV or video-game violence on our behavior, the emphasis is usually on viewer aggression. Thus, we get mental images of a child watching or playing a "shoot-'em-up" sequence full of blood and gore, and then heading to school to beat up some peers on the playground. The study we describe here, however, is a little different because the emphasis is on cooperation versus exploitation in a social situation. And in this case, the video game increased the odds of deciding to take advantage of someone else; cooperation was undermined.

We think two points need to be made here. First, no one should be surprised that kids learn from TV and from video games. The degree to which this learning will truly become part of a consistent pattern of behavior, however, will depend on other aspects of their environment, and that is where parents come in. A frustrated, rejected, alienated kid is very likely to be strongly influenced by antisocial acts on TV or in a video game. The kid from a warm, nurturing, supportive family, on the other hand, is not.

Country singer Rodney Atkins touches on this distinction in a song noting how his young son let out a cuss word. (It began with "S," by the way! This IS a country song!) When asked how he learned to talk like that, the boy replied, "I been watchin' you Dad!" But later, when the boy offers up an eloquent bedtime prayer to God, Rodney asks him where he learned to pray like that. The reply? "I been watchin' you Dad!" In which direction do you think this kid is heading?

How about the best example of them all—Ralphie, from *A Christmas Story*. In this delightful classic movie that millions have made required viewing every

Christmas, Ralphie not only lets out the dreaded "F" word, but he also beats the tar out of the neighborhood bully. Of course, he learned a lot of that behavior by watching his old man. But we bet that no viewer alive would describe Ralphie's basic home environment as cold or rejecting, or predict that he will grow up to be some antisocial terror. Quite to the contrary, we imagine most viewers would predict that Ralphie will become quite a productive member of society with a solid social conscience.

This prediction brings us to our second point. Sure, we should be aware of the influence of media violence on young kids, and we should work to restrain violence. We need to remember, though, that larger environmental influences can counter the potential negative impact of media portrayals. Thus, we should be concerned when we see a child who accepts media violence as an accurate depiction of reality, identifies with violent characters, and believes that violent and aggressive behavior is the way to resolve conflict. In this situation, the child's overall environment is supporting and reinforcing inappropriate media messages.

TV violence is not the enemy responsible for antisocial behavior. The enemies are the parent who yells, "Can't you see I'm busy? Go watch TV and get out of my hair"; the lenient juvenile court system that shelters the young offender; the parent who covers up for a child who has broken the law; the substitution of prescription drugs for discipline to control impulsive behavior in children; and a rule system that ties the hands of teachers and school systems and prevents them from exercising credible effective behavior control techniques.

PRIMARY REFERENCE

Sheese, B. E., and W. G. Graziano. 2005. Deciding to defect: The effects of video-game violence on cooperative behavior. *Psychological Science* 16: 354–57.

ADDITIONAL REFERENCES

Anderson, C. A. and B. J. Bushman. 2001. Effects of violent video games on aggressive behavior, aggressive cognition, aggressive affect, physiological arousal, and prosocial behavior: A meta-analytic review of the scientific literature. *Psychological Science* 12: 353–59.

Anderson, C. A., and B. J. Bushman. 2002. Human aggression. *Annual Review of Psychology* 53: 27–51.

Bushman, B. J., and C. A. Anderson. 2002. Violent video games and hostile expectations: A test of the general aggression model. *Personality and Social Psychology Bulletin* 28: 1679–86.

Sherry, J. L. 2001. The effects of violent video games on aggression: A meta-analysis. *Human Communication Research* 27: 409–31.

Weigman, O., and E. G. M. VanSchie. 1998. Video game playing and its relations with aggressive and prosocial behavior. *British Journal of Social Psychology* 37: 367–78.

PART THREE

COPS, ROBBERS, AND FORENSICS

20
Are Lineups Valid for Identifying Suspects?

If you watch a TV show like *Law and Order* you know the drill. A victim stands in a room and looks through a one-way mirror into an adjoining room. In that room stand about five people who resemble each other, and who are also dressed similarly. The people, of course, have been chosen on the basis of eyewitness reports of physical characteristics and type of dress of the perpetrator. The eyewitness must choose that member of the lineup who is the actual perpetrator.

Now let's picture two scenarios. Imagine one victim who says, "Gee, you know I'm not totally sure here. Number 5 sure looks like him, but it could be number 3, too. You know what? I'm going with number 5." Not exactly a dead-on identification, is it?

But how about this comment: "Oh, it's number 5! He's the one! I would never forget that face and those eyes. I am sure—number 5!" Hang that SOB! He's obviously guilty!

QUESTION: *When victims are more confident in choosing a perpetrator out of a lineup, is their accuracy higher?*
RESEARCH ANSWER: *No.*

ANALYSIS

Confidence when identifying someone in a lineup does not guarantee accuracy. There are just too many factors that influence a victim's confidence in choosing a perpetrator from a lineup that have little to do with their accuracy. For instance, when an eyewitness is praised after identifying a suspect ("Good job! Thanks very much!"), the eyewitness will have more confidence about being correct. Studies have also shown that if eyewitnesses are repeatedly questioned about possible mistakes when they describe their memory, for some reason they become more confident about the memory. It's almost as if some eyewitnesses dig in their heels and rebel against the authority figure (the officer), saying "There's no way my memory is mistaken."

The composition of the lineup is a big factor in confidence. Suppose you're looking at a lineup and there's a person (innocent) in there who is a virtual twin of the actual perpetrator (who is not in the lineup). Studies show you will not only choose the innocent person as the perpetrator, but will do so with an extremely high degree of confidence. The innocent look-alike is screwed!

Studies also show that the eyewitness's confidence about accuracy is influenced by officials administering the lineup. Expectations can be passed on to the witness in subtle and unintended ways, and feedback from officials present can greatly increase confidence but not accuracy. Think about it. When witnesses are viewing a lineup, they probably want to help out. The police, meanwhile, want to wrap up the case and move on. Everyone will be just thrilled when the witness can identify, with "complete confidence," the perpetrator. Everyone is happy, that is, except the poor schlep who is really innocent.

PRIMARY REFERENCE
Wells, G. L., E. A. Olson, and S. D. Charman. 2002. The confidence of eyewitnesses in their identifications from lineups. *Current Directions in Psychological Science* 11: 151–54.

ADDITIONAL REFERENCES

Bradfield, S. L., G. L. Wells, and E. A. Olson. 2002. The damaging effect of confirming feedback on the relation between eyewitness certainty and identification accuracy. *Journal of Applied Psychology* 87: 112–20.

Wells, G. L., R. S. Malpass, R. C. L. Lindsay, R. P. Fisher, J. W. Turtle, S. M. Fulero. 2000. From the lab to the police station: A successful application of eyewitness research. *American Psychologist* 55: 581–98.

Wells, G. L., and E. A. Olson. 2002. Eyewitness identification: Information gain from incriminating and exonerating behaviors. *Journal of Experimental Psychology: Applied* 8: 155–67.

21
Do Other Races All Look the Same?

In any sitcom that deals with people of different races or ethnic groups, the comment will eventually come: "You people all look the same to me!" Well, the next time you hear a joke with that punch line, be prepared; it's true!

QUESTION: *Is it easier for us to recognize members of our racial or ethnic "in-group" than members of the "out-group"?*
RESEARCH ANSWER: *Yes ... but.*

ANALYSIS

Research shows that we tend to perceive members of other racial and ethnic groups, our so-called out-group, as being more homogeneous and harder to tell apart than members of our "in-group." But ... there's a fly in the ointment (there usually is in issues of psychology), and that's why we kind of hedged on our research answer. Let's consider a recent study.

Joshua Ackerman and his colleagues at Arizona State University had white college students look at pictures of whites and blacks. Some of the pictures showed a neutral expression, and some of the pictures showed an angry expression. Next, the students watched a 5-minute film clip that served as a distractor task. Finally, after the film clip, they were given a series of pictures to look at and decide either "yes" (I definitely saw this picture before) or "no" (I did not see this picture before).

If the facial expression depicted in the picture was neutral, the expected result occurred: memory of whether the picture was in the initial list was more accurate for the pictures of whites (in-group) than for blacks (out-group). The results changed, however, if the picture depicted an angry facial expression. In fact, the white subjects showed more accurate memory for the angry black pictures than for the angry white pictures. Thus, if the expressions depicted anger, memory for the out-group was better than for the in-group—precisely the opposite of what was found when the picture expressions were neutral.

If you think about this finding, it makes some sense. An angry expression on someone else conveys a threat of danger to the observer. When threatened, our brains no doubt mobilize and focus, and one example of such focusing is a type of "hardening" of the visual image of the angry person into our brains, making the image more memorable and less prone to forgetting. This hardening of the image might also be strengthened by stereotypes the person holds, such as a white feeling that "all blacks are a threat to me." We're not using very scientific terminology, of course, but you get the idea.

Like any research finding, Ackerman's will need further study. However, the potential relevance of this finding is huge. For example, defense attorneys are well aware of research showing the difficulty in recognizing members of the "out-group." Thus, when a white victim "identifies" a black as the attacker, a defense lawyer can suggest doubt about the accuracy of the identification by citing research we mentioned earlier. They all look alike! But we now have a study saying memory inaccuracies for the out-group are canceled out when an angry expression is present. A prosecutor, therefore, can point out that because a victim's attacker was no doubt showing an angry and aggressive expression, the victim's memory is quite reliable! It's a lot for a jury to sort out, but you are ready to lead class discussion and write an exceptional paper on this issue. If you're on that jury, by the way, you will be master of the courtroom, too!

PRIMARY REFERENCE

Ackerman, J. M., J. R. Shapiro, S. L. Neuberg, D. T. Kenrick, D. Vaughn Becker, V. Griskevicius, J. K. Maner, and M. Schaller. 2006. They all look the same to me (unless they're angry). *Psychological Science* 17: 836–40.

ADDITIONAL REFERENCES

Chance, J. E., and A. G. Goldstein. 1996. The other-race effect and eyewitness identification. In *Psychological Issues in Eyewitness Identification,* edited by S. L. Sporer and R. S. Malpass (153–76). Hillsdale, NJ: Erlbaum.

Chiao, J. Y., H. E. Heck, K. Nakayama, and N. Ambady. Priming race in biracial observers affects visual search for black and white faces. *Psychological Science* 17: 387–92.

Johnson, K. J., and B. L. Fredrickson. 2005. "We all look the same to me": Positive emotions eliminate the own-race bias in face recognition. *Psychological Science* 16: 875–81.

Meissner, C. A., and J. C. Brigham. 2001. Thirty years of investigating the own-race bias in memory for faces: A meta-analytic review. *Psychology, Public Policy, and Law* 7: 3–35.

Shaller. M., J. H. Park, and A. Mueller. 2003. Fear of the dark: Interactive effects of beliefs about danger and ambient darkness on ethnic stereotypes. *Personality and Social Psychology Bulletin* 29: 637–49.

22
Can We Trust the Eyewitness?

In our last two sections we looked at problems with identifying suspects in lineups and at complications that come up when we're trying to remember faces that are the same or different race. The issues we looked at are relevant to an even broader question about how much we should rely on eyewitnesses to an event. Having an eyewitness to a crime, of course, is the holy grail of police investigation; if someone saw the suspect in the act, well ... that pretty much closes the case, right?

QUESTION: *Are eyewitness accounts reliable?*
RESEARCH ANSWER: *No.*

ANALYSIS

Remember, we're not dealing here with how accurate or confident a witness is when selecting someone out of lineup, or with accuracy identifying someone who is of another race. We're simply asking if we trust an eyewitness's description of what actually happened. "Tell me what you saw." Can we trust what the eyewitness says?

Several years ago one of us was walking down the street approaching an intersection. A look ahead showed that the traffic light was changing from yellow to red, too soon to get across the street. Suddenly, to the right, there was a screeching of brakes and a loud crash. "I looked over and it was quite clear that this guy had tried to run the red light, and crashed into a car that had the green and had proceeded into the intersection from the left of the guy running the light. The victim was solidly broadsided."

Later that evening, your keen observing author went to the police station to give his official account of the accident. Using a street diagram, he was halfway through his description when the officer stopped him and said, "That's not the direction the car that was hit was going. He was coming from the other direction and attempting to make a left turn as the light was turning red, and the car coming at him went into him."

"Really?" your sharp-eyed psychologist replied. "Well, either way, the other guy ran the red light."

We wonder what would have happened if that accident had gone to trial, and your author had to testify. We have no doubt that the eyewitness account would have been totally decimated by even a semicompetent defense attorney:

> Now let me get this straight, sir. You say the plaintiff's car was heading into the intersection with the green light, and was broadsided by my client. But how can that be when the plaintiff was heading in the opposite direction as my client, and attempting to make a left turn? You didn't see this accident at all, did you? You saw two cars sitting in the intersection after the crash and simply assumed what had happened. In fact, isn't it entirely likely that the plaintiff cut off my client?

Eyewitness? Yeh, right! This so-called eyewitness account was quite distorted and inaccurate. Don't get us wrong; the guy did run the red light. The one making the left turn, however, mistakenly assumed the runner would be stopping, allowing him to complete his turn. They were probably both at fault, but the point is that the eyewitness believed that the one who was hit was moving into the intersection with a green light.

Psychologists have studied the dynamics of eyewitness accounts for decades. The name most associated with research over the last 30 years is Elizabeth Loftus, and her 1979 book *Eyewitness Testimony* remains relevant. Loftus and many other researchers have given us study after study showing how the accounts of eyewitnesses can be influenced by a variety of extraneous factors. Let's just list some of the things that appear to produce errors. Remember, these findings are from carefully conducted and controlled studies that show participants pictures or videotapes of staged crimes, or actually stage an event in front of the subject.

- The chance of a mistake is greater in other-race compared to same-race situations. This fact shouldn't surprise us because we have already seen that it is harder to identify people whose race is different from the observer, at least when the observer does not feel threatened.

- The more violent a crime, the less accurate the eyewitness account. This finding is usually interpreted as showing the influence of stress on the observer;

increases in stress decrease accuracy when trying to remember the exact sequence of events and other details surrounding the event.

- The presence of a weapon can divert an observer's attention and reduce accuracy.

- As expected, the more time a witness has to observe a crime, the greater the accuracy in identifying the perpetrator. Coverings like hats and hoods, or disguises like beards, wigs, and mustaches, however, can cancel out this exposure effect.

- The longer the delay between the crime and the identification, the lower the accuracy. The trail goes cold.

- The way questions are posed and the words used in interviewing witnesses can influence their memory and accuracy. In the past 15 years, efforts have been made to improve witness questioning by developing a standard structured interview procedure that reflects known cognitive principles from psychological research. This procedure, known as the Cognitive Interview, has been extensively studied and often increases accurate eyewitness accounts. Unfortunately, the method is not widely used.

Let's remember that becoming aware of the many factors that can influence witnesses does not mean we should discount everything the witness says. Quite to the contrary, the point of research in this area is to identify relevant factors so that law enforcement authorities can develop techniques to minimize the likelihood of errors. The goal is to reduce false identification of the innocent and increase correct identification of the guilty. Thus, when we hear an eyewitness report, our automatic response should not be, "Well, I know how wrong eyewitnesses can be so I'm not going to believe your account." Rather, we should examine the conditions surrounding the event itself, and the procedures by which the eyewitness is reporting recollections, and then decide on the likelihood that we may be dealing with inaccuracies.

PRIMARY REFERENCE

Wells, G. L., A. Memon, and S. D. Penrod. 2006. Eyewitness evidence: Improving its probative value. *Psychological Science in the Public Interest* 7: 45–75.

ADDITIONAL REFERENCES

Davies, G. M., and T. Valentine. 2006. Facial composites: Forensic utility and psychological research. In *Handbook of Eyewitness Psychology, Vol. 2*, edited by R.C.L. Lindsay, D. F. Ross, J. D. Read, and M. P. Toglia (59–86). Mahwah, NJ: Erlbaum.

Loftus, E. 1979. *Eyewitness Testimony*. Cambridge, MA: Harvard University Press.

Wells, G. L., and L. E. Hasel. 2007. Facial composite production by eyewitnesses. *Current Directions in Psychological Science* 16: 6–10.

Wells, G. L., and E. Olson. 2003. Eyewitness identification. *Annual Review of Psychology* 54: 277–95.

23
Do Black Facial Features Arouse Bias in White Juries?

In an earlier section, we saw how recognition of faces is easier when we're looking at someone who is a member of our racial "in-group." We also pointed out that this finding tends to disappear when the out-group face is expressing anger. Thus, for a white person, seeing angry black faces facilitates accurate future recognition, possibly because the angry expression taps into fears about becoming the victim of physical harm.

Psychologists have also studied race as a factor in reaching jury decisions. Ideally, of course, jurors are supposed to reach decisions based on the facts of a case, on the evidence presented during the trial. Unfortunately, many studies have shown that race is a powerful factor influencing jurors when they determine the guilt or innocence of a defendant. And blacks usually come out on the short end.

QUESTION: *Is race a factor in death-penalty cases?*
RESEARCH ANSWER: *Yes.*

ANALYSIS

Black defendants are more likely than whites to receive a death sentence in capital cases. Furthermore, killers of whites are more likely to be sentenced to death than are killers of blacks. There is no doubt that racial bias on juries plays an active role in our judicial system by influencing verdicts. Jennifer Eberhardt of Stanford, and her colleagues at UCLA, Yale, and Cornell, recently presented evidence taking this racial bias one step further. Skin color is only part of the equation; having other stereotypically black facial features stacks the deck against a black defendant even beyond the influence of having dark skin. Such facial features include a broad nose, hair texture, thick lips, and darker skin tone.

The authors prepared standardized photographs of actual black defendants accused of killing a white person. Independent raters, who had no idea who was in the picture, simply rated each photograph according to how stereotypically black the individuals in the picture were. The results showed that the more the person was rated as stereotypically black, the more likely that defendant received a death sentence at the actual trial.

This finding was limited to trials in which the black was being tried for killing a white. When a black was on trial for killing a black, there was no relationship between how much the defendant was rated as possessing stereotypically black characteristics and whether that defendant received the death penalty. So the racial bias works in very subtle ways. Being black is bad enough; but the more you appear black, the more powerfully the negative stereotype kicks in—IF you are accused of killing a white! The stereotype influence does not enter the picture when both the perpetrator and the victim are black.

If nothing else, this study shows that racial bias is both subtle and probably largely unconscious. That is, we doubt a juror is thinking during the trial, "Look at those black features; this guy is definitely guilty, especially because he killed one of my race." Rather, the facial features that are at work here are being processed at a below-conscious level and result from a consistent pattern of racially biased thinking. The fact that the process is so automatic is worrisome, especially for those who might want to be on guard for possible racial prejudice.

Brian Payne of the University of North Carolina provides us with another example of how a racial bias can influence our thinking. While participants looked at a screen, he flashed images on the screen that they had to identify. The images were either a common everyday hand tool or a gun. Just before the picture appeared, Payne also flashed a photo of a person, either black or white. The participants were told to try and ignore the photo, and concentrate on identifying the object that would only appear briefly. Did they see a gun or a hand tool?

Under conditions when the participant had to decide very quickly, within half a second after the item appeared, accurate identification of the gun was better when the gun image was preceded by a picture of a black man. When the gun was preceded by a photo of a white man, more mistakes were made when deciding whether a gun or a hand tool was depicted. By the same token, when a picture of a hand tool was preceded by a photo of a black man, the tool was more likely to be mistakenly identified as a gun.

Let's review a bit and see what we have going on here. First, whites have a hard time distinguishing pictures of blacks unless the expression is angry. Thus, for a white, an angry black face appears to stir strong emotional arousal and defensiveness. We also see that blacks are more likely to be associated with weapons and with a judicial death sentence. These findings are quite consistent and disturbing because they occur in people who have been raised in a presumably enlightened society. These findings suggest that racism is alive and well in our society, a conclusion not at all surprising to many.

Maybe we shouldn't be too hard on ourselves, though. When based on obvious points of difference between members of a species (such as skin color, gender, or obvious ethnicity), prejudice is going to rear its ugly head. And even in outwardly nonprejudiced individuals, latent tendencies toward bias may be awakened. But what really counts is our eventual behavior. An employer in Payne's procedure, for instance, may mistakenly "see" a gun when it's preceded by a black face, but that employer may also hire a lot of blacks in his business. Sure, the guy may have latent hostility toward blacks, but does that count more than his hiring record?

Whatever your feelings in these issues, at least you can be secure in the knowledge that you are prepared for any informal or class discussion that touches on racial prejudice. And, of course, you can also point out that studies tend to look at bias in whites toward blacks. There's not much to say about evidence in the other direction because there's not much research.

PRIMARY REFERENCES

Eberhardt, J. L., P. G. Davies, V. J. Purdie-Vaughns, and S. L. Johnson. 2006. Looking deathworthy: Perceived stereotypicality of Black defendants predicts capital-sentencing outcomes. *Psychological Science* 17: 383–86.

Payne, B. K. 2006. Weapon bias: Split-second decisions and unintended stereotyping. *Current Directions in Psychological Science* 15: 287–91.

ADDITIONAL REFERENCES

Cheryan, S., and G. V. Bodenhausen. 2000. When positive stereotypes threaten intellectual performance: The psychological hazards of "model minority" status. *Psychological Science* 11: 399–402.

Levin, D. T. 2000. Race as a visual feature: Using visual search and perceptual discrimination tasks to understand face categories and the cross-race recognition deficit. *Journal of Experimental Psychology: General* 129: 559–74.

Levin, D. T., and B. L. Angelone. 2002. Categorical perception of race. *Perception* 16: 181–205.

24
What Causes Aggression in the Workplace

Here's a great topic for those of you getting ready to enter the workforce. Consider this scenario: It's break time, and you and your colleagues are gathered around the snack area and the topic of worker violence comes up. Maybe Joe down the hall yelled at someone earlier, or maybe Fran is having a bad day and told everyone to buzz off. Try throwing this question out for consideration:

QUESTION: *Is extreme violence at work most likely to come from someone inside the organization?*
RESEARCH ANSWER: *No.*

ANALYSIS

The fact is, when we're talking about actual killing or a physical assault, most workplace violence comes from an outsider, a member of the public. More than 80 percent of workplace violence comes from an outsider. Employees may yell and spread rumors about each other, but they seldom physically attack or try to kill a co-worker.

When insider aggression does occur in an organization, one or both of two individual factors are usually involved: (1) alcohol and (2) a perception that the organization is unfair and "I am being mistreated." These factors are stronger when the aggressor has low job security. It is important to remember that we're dealing with perceptions here. The individual interprets the workplace as threatening his or her well-being and security. This threat may not be objectively present, but as long as it is perceived as present, it is quite real to the person. For instance, a worker may be overlooked for a promotion because of financial strains in the company. If, however, the worker interprets the nonpromotion as demonstrating that he or she is disliked and should be removed from the company, then the probability of workplace aggression is much higher.

In addition to individual factors, several organizational factors have been linked to inside workplace aggression, such as layoffs, diversity policies, downsizing, drug testing, raising workload, and surveillance. Research also shows company policies that make workers feel they are not treated politely, respectfully, or with dignity will increase the likelihood of workplace aggression from within.

Not surprisingly, studies show considerable negative impact resulting from workplace aggression, whether initiated from an outsider or an insider. When aggression is initiated from the inside, however, the visibility of company policies that may have contributed to the violence is magnified among workers and is especially damaging. Thus, when there is insider aggression, other workers feel a breach of trust and a sense of betrayal from the organization. One of their own has snapped, and it is easy to lay blame with organizational policies. Outsider aggression is less likely to produce this response from workers. Insider aggression will also affect workers' commitment to the organization. Again, it is easier to apply blame directly to employer policies when they appear to affect workers. Employees generally hold the organization more responsible for insider-initiated than outsider-initiated aggression.

The factors leading to workplace aggression are extremely complex and difficult to unravel. One reason is that conditions under which such aggression can occur are so varied. A member of the public with no relationship to the company may merely appear, such as a bank robber. Someone with an association with the company, but still an outsider, may commit the act, such as someone receiving medical treatment or being counseled in a social service agency. The offender could be a current or former worker who has an axe to grind over some perceived mistreatment. The very fact that workplace violence can take place in so many contexts makes it difficult to understand, much less predict.

PRIMARY REFERENCE
LeBlane, M. M., and J. Barling. 2004. Workplace aggression. *Current Directions in Psychology* 13: 9–12.

ADDITIONAL REFERENCES
Douglas, S. S., and M. J. Martinko. 2001. Exploring the role of individual differences in the prediction of workplace aggression. *Journal of Applied Psychology* 86: 547–59.
Durpré, K. E., and J. Barling. 2002. *The prediction and prevention of workplace aggression and violence.* Unpublished manuscript, Memorial University, St. John's, Newfoundland, Canada.
Durpré, K. E., and J. Barling. 2003. Workplace aggression. In *Misbehavior and Dysfunctional Attitudes in Organizations*, edited by A. Sagie, S. Stashevsky, and M. Koslowsky (13–32). New York: Palgrave/Macmillan.
Jockin, V., R. D. Arvey, and M. McGue. 2001. Perceived victimization moderates self-reports of workplace aggression and conflict. *Journal of Applied Psychology* 86: 1262–69.
LeBlanc, M. M., and E. K. Kelloway. 2002. Predictors and outcomes of workplace violence and aggression. *Journal of Applied Psychology* 87: 444–53.

25
When Do Sex Offenders Repeat?

Few crimes in our society raise more emotions and concerns than those involving sex attacks, especially when the victims are children. There also seems to be a prevailing belief among the general public of "once a sexual offender, always a sexual offender." Most of us feel that sexual crimes are not like crimes of opportunity like stealing; theft seems to be a simple case of raising money when one is in need, whereas sex crimes seem to be the result of some irresistible impulse to dominate and control a victim, and throw in a little sexual gratification for the perpetrator along the way. Such impulses, we feel, are probably a core part of one's personality, and not likely to go away, even after treatment. Does this view hold up to scientific scrutiny? In posing our research question, we're going to include a key word, so read carefully.

QUESTION: *Is it inevitable that sex offenders will continue their ways after treatment and punishment?*
RESEARCH ANSWER: *No.*

ANALYSIS

Obviously, the important word in our question is "inevitable." One challenging aspect of psychology is that when we study behavior, we quickly learn that nothing is inevitable; nothing is certain; nothing is guaranteed. That fact makes us chuckle when we hear some behavior expert testify in a courtroom that "This individual is rehabilitated and no longer a danger to society"; or "The individual simply will never be rehabilitated and will always be a danger." We can certainly make educated guesses, but stating such predictions with certainty is shaky. No wonder many courtrooms have become therapists' couches where one expert is pitted against another to convince a jury that the defendant is, or is not, stable.

Karl Hanson of the Solicitor General's Office of Canada presents some actual figures about sex offenders and the likelihood they will continue to offend. The figures are based on 61 studies involving almost 24,000 offenders. Only about 13 percent of sex offenders committed a new sex offense within 4 to 5 years following release from prison. The new offense rate for rapists was 22 percent and for child molesters, 10 percent. If we look, however, at the likelihood of the sex offender committing *any* new offense, the percentage rises to 36 percent.

The low rate for child offenders (10 percent) is particularly interesting because it is precisely in this area that many of us feel "once a child molester, always a child molester." We believe a sexual and/or an emotional attraction to children is not likely to change after prison or treatment; the attraction is ingrained, just as our personal sexual identification is ingrained and not likely to change.

A couple of comments are in order here. First of all, the percentages mentioned are based on a 4- to 5-year period. Once we extend that period to 20 years the percentage of those recommitting the same crime increases substantially to nearly 40 percent. Also, a new crime committed by a sex offender might never be recorded. Thus, the percentages are very likely underestimations. In spite of these cautions, however, many researchers feel the evidence is clear in showing that, on average, nonsexual offenders are more likely to commit new crimes after imprisonment than are sexual offenders.

That last conclusion in itself is probably good enough to gain you some stature as someone knowledgeable about behavior. You also need to point out, however, that risk factors can enter the picture and increase the likelihood of repeat offenses for sex crime perpetrators. When we throw in these risk factors, we begin to see that many circumstances are more consistent with the "they don't change" belief among the public.

- The strongest risk factor for committing a new sex crime is when the victims are children. Pedophiles show a greater than 50 percent likelihood of continuing their behavior following imprisonment.

- Another strong risk factor is when the sex crime involves a deviancy of any sort. Examples of deviancies might be targeting a specific gender, a specific age, or a specific occupation; acts requiring more than mere intercourse can also be included in this risk category.

- Preying on strangers as victims is more of a risk factor for repeat offenses than is an episode with an acquaintance or relative.

- Antisocial personality dysfunctions like sociopathy are definite risk factors.

- The more prior offenses, the greater the risk for new crimes. This factor, of course, begs the question, "OK, this offense is the first one for this particular perpetrator, but will it be the first in what is to be a long series?"

- General criminal lifestyle, a young age, and a history of juvenile delinquency are notable risk factors.

- Sex offenders typically suffer from anxiety disorders, depression, and low self-esteem. These factors in and of themselves, however, are certainly not markers for sex crimes.

Once we throw in these risk factors, we can truly refine our educated guesses about the likelihood of a repeat offender. Thus, if we have a depressed 30-year-old pedophile with a history of run-ins with the law and a tendency toward deviant sexual behaviors, we're not talking about a risk factor of 10 percent. In fact, combining risk factors can result in a fairly high prediction accuracy for the likelihood of a repeat offender.

PRIMARY REFERENCE

Hanson, R. K. 2000. Will they do it again? Predicting sex-offense recidivism. *Current Directions in Psychological Science* 9: 106–9.

ADDITIONAL REFERENCES

Hanson, R. K. 1998. What do we know about sex offender risk assessment? *Psychology, Public Policy, and Law 4:* 50–72.

Hanson, R. K., and M. T. Bussière. 1998. Predicting relapse: A meta-analysis of sexual offender recidivism studies. *Journal of Consulting and Clinical Psychology* 66: 348–62.

Hanson, R. K., and A. J. R. Harris. 2000. Where should we intervene? Dynamic predictors of sex offense recidivism. *Criminal Justice and Behavior* 27: 6–35.

Hanson, R. K., and D. Thornton. 2000. Improving risk assessments for sex offenders: A comparison of three actuarial scales. *Law and Human Behavior* 24: 119–36.

Quinsey, V. L., M. L. Lalumière, M. E. Rice, and G. T. Harris. 1995. Predicting sexual offenses. In *Assessing Dangerousness: Violence by Sexual Offenders, Batterers, and Child Abusers*, edited by J. C. Campbell (114–137). Thousand Oaks, CA: Sage.

26
Do Terrorists Show a Common Personality Profile?

Most of us like to believe that there are some standard causes for terrorism. How many of us want to say something like, "We know they're all nuts, of course; they probably suffer from some personality disorder and need to be on Zoloft or some other miracle drug we hear about every day on TV. Also, we're often told that they have frustrating lives, suffering from economic hardship or political oppression. These common factors probably are the reason our government can profile these characters."

Profiling! There's something that grabs our attention. The media seems eager to tell us about airport profiling to identify potential terrorists—how they walk, their expression, eye movements, and the like. (These media stories, of course, tell us how to avoid looking like a terrorist! We can only hope that those who would do us harm don't pay attention!)

A few years ago the United States Secret Service did a comprehensive study of every known assassin or attacker of a prominent government official. The goal was to see if there is a profile common to assassins through the years. The conclusion? Sorry, life isn't that simple. Whereas many assassins have a few things in common, any attempt to draw up a standard profile for assassins would be futile; there is just too much variation in personality dynamics, family background, life trauma, and current life circumstances to rely on a profile to identify potential assassins.

In any event, looking for common personalities and backgrounds for terrorists is similar to profiling. So....

QUESTION: *Is there a standard personality type and/or an environmental background for terrorists who want to destroy Western civilization?*
RESEARCH ANSWER: *No.*

ANALYSIS

According to Arie Kruglanski and Shira Fishman of the University of Maryland, research has yet to show any unique personality makeup for terrorists. Of course, in a given individual, an unstable psychological makeup could be one of many causes for terrorist actions, but that fact does not mean that other terrorists will show similar unstable characteristics.

Are terrorists aggressive? Impulsive? Narcissistic? Loners? Depressed? Anxious? Frustrated? We could go on and on and answer ''yes'' to many factors on our list when looking at individuals. But if you want to compile a checklist of 10 items and say, ''This guy got six checks and therefore he's probably a terrorist!''—Well, you're going to strike out a lot.

By the same token, factors like poverty, a decaying environment, poor education, unstable family life, and political oppression do not provide us with a unique background profile for terrorists. There simply is no standardized list of root causes that are going to emerge in an analysis of terrorists.

Many psychologists say that because the search for personality and background profiles is not fruitful, we should analyze terrorism as a tool, a weapon, a method to get something the terrorist wants. Rich or poor, educated or not, oppressed or not—anyone can choose to use terrorism as a tactic to obtain something wanted.

This view of terrorism, of course, suggests that the best way to fight it is to convince potential terrorists that they are wrong, that their tactic will not work, or at least that it is not worth the effort. Of course, this process is not as easy as it sounds because some terrorists are crazy enough to strap a nuclear bomb to their chest and walk to the center of Manhattan. Many Homeland Security officials say it is because of these extremists that we must use every means at our disposal to protect ourselves.

But what of the person or organization that views terrorism as one of several potential ways (such as diplomacy, negotiations, media propaganda campaigns) of obtaining gains? In this case, strategies to convince such an organization that the option of terrorism is not a likely way to gain their goals might have some effect.

One thing seems clear. Psychological analysis tells us that terrorism is a multifaceted phenomenon. Identifying which facet we may be dealing with in a particular case may help us adjust our strategies to counter it in effective ways.

PRIMARY REFERENCE

Kruglanski, A. W., and S. Fishman. 2006. Terrorism between "syndrome" and "tool." *Current Directions in Psychological Science* 15: 45–48.

ADDITIONAL REFERENCES

Carr, C. 2003. *The Lesson of Terror: A History Of Warfare against Civilizations.* New York: Random House.

Gunaratna, R. 2002. *Inside Al Qaeda: Global Network of Terror.* New York: Columbia University Press.

Horgan, J. 2005. *The Psychology of Terrorism.* London: Routledge.

Krueger, A. B., and J. Malexkova. 2002, June 24. Does poverty cause terrorism? *The New Republic* 226: 27–33.

McCauley, C. (in press). Psychological issue in understanding terrorism and the response to terrorism. In *The Psychology of Terrorism,* edited by C. Stout. Westport, CT: Greenwood Publishing.

PART FOUR

MEMORY AND INTELLIGENCE

27
How Well Do We Remember Our Past?

All of us have probably had the experience of chatting with an elderly parent or a grandparent and being fascinated while they shared with us some memory from the past. They tell the story confidently, in rich detail, and we generally accept the story as part of family lore and tradition until we mention the story to another elderly relative, who says, "Oh, that's not what happened at all! What you heard is wrong. Let me tell you what really happened."

Where do these contradictory stories leave us? Who is right? Both? Neither? Is the truth somewhere in the middle? We'll never know for sure, but at least we can ask if psychological research has anything to say about the reliability of memories in the elderly.

QUESTION: *Are memories of older people accurate?*
RESEARCH ANSWER: *No.*

ANALYSIS
A variety of studies have been done showing that distortions of memory are more likely to occur in older subjects (usually defined as over 65). To illustrate one type of study, imagine that you sat down with your 68-year-old uncle and read him a list of words. In that list, the word "building" was repeated three times. "Mountain," on the other hand, only occurred once.

Next, you read a list of words to uncle and tell him to concentrate on them because you will ask him to remember them later. "Building," by the way, is *not* in this second list. Finally, you read your uncle a list of words and ask him if each word appeared in the second list. You even warn him that a word from the first list may appear, and he should reject it as appearing in the second list.

What happens is that the more times a word was repeated in the first list (remember, "building" was repeated three times, "mountain" only once), the more likely uncle is to claim it was in the second list. Thus, uncle is more likely to claim that "building" appeared in the second list than did "mountain." Uncle's memory for the second list is more likely to be distorted by repetition of a word in the first list than when the word is only stated once in the first list.

Our little anecdote with the uncle is offered as an example of what is found in formal research. Older participants' memory for material is distorted when that material has been repeated more than once. That result, by the way, is not found for young research participants.

The influence of repetition is especially noteworthy because when we hear a story from an old relative, that story has likely been told and retold many times. Each time the version is probably changed just a wee bit, but with each repetition, the now distorted memory of what actually happened is incorporated into the person's memory; as far as they are concerned, the distorted version is what actually happened.

Here's another interesting technique researchers use to measure memory accuracy. Suppose you give your uncle a list of words that have a theme: football, outfield, first base, yard line, umpire, end zone, goalkeeper, referee—you get the idea; all these words are related to sports. The actual word "sports," however, is not one of the words. Later, let's give uncle (who's probably a little tired of being your guinea pig at this point!) a list of words and ask him if each one was in the original list. He is very like to identify "sports" as one of the original words.

Again, in formal research studies this result is precisely what is found with old, but not with young participants. The next time someone says to you, "I have a 90-year-old grandfather and he's sharp as a tack," offer up a little cautionary tidbit. Many studies show that older people are very prone to distortions of memory even though they are confident in the accuracy of those memories. Grandpa may spin a good yarn for you from the old days, but that story may be full of distortions. Grandpa will be confident he is correct, even though Grandma says he's full of it!

Enough of this elderly bashing! How about young adults? Are their memories necessarily accurate? To answer this question, we're going to phrase a second research question in a particular way:

QUESTION: *Do our current emotions influence our memories of past events?*
RESEARCH ANSWER: *Yes.*

ANALYSIS

Linda Levine and Martin Safer of the University of California, Irvine, report studies showing how one's current emotional state can distort memories of how we felt at a previous time. For example, shortly after the O. J. Simpson verdict, people were asked how angry they felt. Two months later, they were asked if they thought O. J. was guilty (the verdict was "innocent") and were asked to recall how angry they felt when they heard the verdict. Note that this procedure allows the researchers to compare actual level of anger with the memory of the level of anger. The results showed that those who currently felt O. J. was guilty *overestimated* how angry they remembered feeling. In other words, they remembered themselves as being angrier than they actually were at the time they heard the verdict.

In another study, before taking a test, college students were asked how nervous they were. A couple of weeks later, before returning the test, the professor told the students they either did well or poorly on the test. (What they were told was determined randomly and was not based on how well the students actually did on the test.) Then, before the students could look at their test, the professor asked them to indicate how nervous they remembered feeling before the test. Once again, note how the procedure allowed the researchers to compare the actual level of pretest anxiety with the level remembered some time later. The results showed that the students who were told they did well on the test *underestimated* how anxious they truly were at the time of the test; similarly, the students told they did poorly on the test *overestimated* how anxious they felt before the test.

Results like these suggest that our memories are used to reconstruct our past to make the past consistent with how we currently feel. Past discomfort can be forgotten or reduced in our minds if we are no longer in distress. On the other hand, if we are presently in discomfort or distress, we have a tendency to remember our earlier distress as greater than it actually was. Let's not be too harsh on Grandpa, therefore, when he spins yarns of yesterday. After all, it appears that memory distortions can occur at any age.

PRIMARY REFERENCES

Jacoby, L. L., and M. G. Rhodes. 2006. False remembering in the aged. *Current Directions in Psychological Science* 15: 49–53.
Levine, L. J., and M. A. Safer. 2002. Sources of bias in memory for emotions. *Current Directions in Psychological Science* 11: 169–73.

ADDITIONAL REFERENCES

Conway, M. A., and C. W. Pleydell-Pearce. 2000. The construction of autobiographical memories in the self-memory system. *Psychological Review* 107: 261–88.

Fredrickson, B. L. 2000. Extracting meaning from past affective experiences: The importance of peaks, ends, and specific emotions. *Cognition and Emotion* 14: 577–606.

Marsh, E. J. 2007. Retelling is not the same as recalling. *Current Directions in Psychological Science* 16: 16–20.

Loftus, E. F. 1992. When a lie becomes memory's truth: Memory distortion after exposure to misinformation. *Current Directions in Psychological Science* 1: 121–23.

Safer, M. A., and D. J. Keuler. 2002. Individual differences in misremembering pre-psychotherapy distress: Personality and memory distortion. *Emotion* 2: 162–78.

28
Are Adult Memories of Childhood Sexual Abuse Reliable?

Let's set up a hypothetical situation. Fran is in therapy. She doesn't think she has any serious fundamental psychological problems, but her life isn't what she wants it to be. She's 38, married, and has a couple of kids, ages 11 and 13. Fran feels unhappy now and then, and has some bouts of anxiety that she just can't explain. She doesn't get along that well with either of her parents, who live 200 miles away, and sees them only at Christmas. She works and is fairly satisfied with her job as an executive secretary. Things are pretty stable in the marriage, although she feels her husband wants to play golf and hang out with his guy buddies more than with her. She sees more and more conflict popping up with the kids. One big problem is that she and her husband usually disagree on how to restrict and discipline the kids, who are beginning to spread their wings.

Fran's friends, like many of us, consider her unhappiness and discomfort about her life stress and adjustment challenges to be depression. This word, "depression," is casually used in our everyday conversation. We eagerly apply it to people like Fran who are unhappy and stressed about various problems in life. The fact is, however, that being unhappy does not necessarily mean one is depressed. Furthermore, unhappiness is often caused by events that we can confront, challenge, and change. Fran, for instance, would do well to discuss her feelings directly with her husband, and insist he cut back on his golfing, and that they come to some agreement about disciplining the children.

Fran's friends, however, see her as depressed, and they keep telling her about the wonderful antidepressants and anti-anxiety medications on the market. Fran, of course, also sees these products advertised all the time on TV. But she doesn't want to go the drug route; she is aware that many of her difficulties are things she can work to change, and she wants to get some insight into why she gets down so often, and why she feels so anxious and uncertain in so many situations. She especially wants to learn how to manage the conflicts she has with her kids, and she would like to have a better relationship with her parents. She decides to see a psychologist and to get involved in regular therapy sessions.

Therapy seems to be going along pretty well. Then, during her fourth session, her therapist asks, "This thing about your parents—what do you remember about your childhood?" She proceeds to recall and talk about various experiences, all of which seem pretty normal to her.

At one point the therapist asks, "This conflict with your father you still have. Usually, those things begin in childhood. Do you remember any specific discomfort you had with him when you were really young, say around 5 or 6? Do you recall any episodes where, maybe, he behaved inappropriately toward you? Maybe touched you the wrong way, or got you all confused because of the way he treated you?''

Fran responds in a very adamant fashion: "If you're asking did my father abuse me in some sexual way, the answer is most definitely no. No way. I have no memory of anything like that, nor do I even remotely believe that such things ever happened.''

The psychologist replies: "That's interesting. Often, when clients like you who have absolutely no memory of anything inappropriate between them and a parent, that lack of memory indicates that something indeed did happen; the memory is so unpleasant it has been repressed—banished from the conscious mind. And you're so sure—again, the intensity of your response can suggest that some repressive blocks are at work.''

Fran says, "You mean to tell me that because I can't remember my father abused me suggests he did!''

"That's often the case," the therapist replies. "I think we should at least entertain the possibility and delve more deeply into some of your memories. You might be surprised at what we uncover.''

If you think this conversation is preposterous, don't! You would be surprised, especially a few years ago, how many therapists tried to link psychological conflicts in adults to sexual abuse by a parent when they were children. Many therapists' efforts were often successful, and their clients "bought into" the interpretation that the cause of their problems was parental sexual abuse. (We should note that such therapist behavior was not typical and is frowned upon by the psychology profession.)

Why would a client so easily begin to accept the possibility of parental sexual abuse? Well, think about it. When people go into therapy, they are usually looking for answers. They are somewhat unstable, adrift psychologically, and they are extremely vulnerable to anything the therapist says. In fact, it's often very difficult to question or challenge the therapist. So here they are, looking for answers to their problems. They have taken a major step of initiating therapy and they want to believe the therapy will help them. In other words, a lot of psychological mental machinery is in motion that will encourage them to accept interpretations offered by the therapist. Once the possibility of childhood sexual abuse is suggested, the mental seed is planted and many (not all, thank goodness!) clients find themselves thinking, "Hmmm. Maybe there's something to this. Maybe dad/mom did cross the line. One thing for sure, if it's true and I confront the accused, I'll be a lot better off!''

QUESTION: *When an adult in therapy begins to remember episodes of childhood sexual abuse, should we be skeptical that the memory is valid?*
RESEARCH ANSWER: *Yes.*

ANALYSIS

First of all, let's think back to the previous section and say again that we should be skeptical of any adult memory of childhood. Memories are not like digital files stored on a CD; our memory systems are like a river bottom that constantly shifts and changes in response to variations in river currents. Every time we have a new experience, our memories can be influenced and modified to fall into line with the new experience.

Studies have even shown that false memories of childhood events can be implanted! It appears that about 25 percent of us are suggestible enough that we can be made to incorporate a nonexistent childhood event (e.g., getting lost in a store when we were 4, or being hospitalized overnight for a high fever, or getting too rambunctious at a relative's wedding and knocking over a table) into our memories and actually come to believe that the event truly happened. Findings like these should make us all pause when we reflect on the validity of our memories.

As we saw in the previous section, studies have also shown that our current level of satisfaction with our lives will influence our memories of the past. For instance, remember that students who were told they did well on a test tended to remember themselves as less anxious before the test than they actually were; conversely, students who were told they did poorly on a test tended to remember themselves as more anxious before the test than they actually were. Findings like these should not surprise us. After all, find someone who is depressed and ask them about childhood events; we doubt you'll get many "Brady-Bunch, all-the-fun-times-I-had" replies.

Elke Geraerts of Maastricht University, The Netherlands, and colleagues at Harvard and elsewhere recently put a somewhat different slant on the memory issue. They were able to form three groups of women who were in their late 30s to early 40s: (a) those who said they had experienced, as adults, a recovered memory of childhood sexual abuse, a memory they said they had originally forgotten; (b) those who said they were victims of childhood sexual abuse and had never forgotten the incidents; and (c) those who said they were not victims of sexual abuse.

The researchers gave the women a series of memory tests. The results showed some interesting differences in memory processing for the women who claimed they had been victims of sexual abuse as children, but subsequently forgot the incidents before recovering the memory later as an adult. Specifically, in the experiment itself, these women tended to forget that they had successfully recalled learned material during the experiment. In other words, at one stage of the experiment, these women thought they had forgotten material learned earlier in the experiment, when in fact they had not forgotten it. They were under a mistaken impression. Applying this result to their actual lives, it becomes possible that when these women "remembered" their early childhood sexual abuse, they were overestimating the degree to which they had ever forgotten the experiences. They believed that at one point in their life they didn't remember the abuse, when in fact that forgetting never really did take place! This is a particularly fascinating finding.

In a later study, Geraerts and her colleagues provide us with some interesting data that show another aspect of the problem with adults remembering sexual abuse when a child. The researchers conducted extensive interviews and testing with adults who claimed they had recovered memories of earlier sexual abuse. They also interviewed family members and friends. The researchers were able to identify two groups of people who had suddenly recovered forgotten memories of sexual abuse: those who recovered their memory of the abuse during formal psychotherapy, and those who suddenly remembered abuse episodes but were not undergoing any sort of psychological treatment at the time.

The researchers could find little objective confirmation of the memories for those who recovered them during therapy. That is, extensive interviewing and investigation with relatives and friends just did not verify the events these people said they suddenly began to remember during therapy sessions. Also, these clients said they did not feel very surprised when the memories came flooding back; it's as if they were there all along. The researchers concluded that the lack of the confirming facts, plus the fact the clients were not surprised at the recovered memory, indicated that suggestions during therapy sessions were having a cumulative effect and the clients were slowly buying into these suggestions from the therapist.

How about those who recovered memories during the regular course of their lives, and not in any context of therapy? In these cases, the researchers were more likely to find confirming evidence that the forgotten sexual abuse actually did take place. Let's be cautious, here! We're not talking 100 percent confirmation, and we're not referring to evidence that would meet the criterion of "beyond reasonable doubt" required in a criminal court trial. All we're saying is that, statistically, more cases of actual abuse could be verified when the memory was recovered outside of therapy than during therapy.

Let's remember that we would never say there are no folks who, as adults, genuinely recover a memory of childhood sexual abuse that at one point in their lives they just do not recall. We are saying, however, that for the most part, this is not the manner in which our memory systems work. When an adult suddenly remembers, "Yes, it's all coming back to me now! I was abused as a child," we should raise the red flag and be cautious, especially if the memory recovery took place during formal therapy. There are too many factors that could lead the person to accept the abuse as real. Under the influence of a therapist, the person could be grasping at straws to gain some closure. Another possibility is that the person could be forgetting that the event was really never forgotten!

PRIMARY REFERENCE

Geraerts, E., M. M. Arnold, D. S. Lindsay, H. Merckelbach, M. Jelicic, and B. Hauer. 2007. The reality of recovered memories: Corroborating continuous and discontinuous memories of childhood sexual abuse. *Psychological Science* 18: 564–68.

ADDITIONAL REFERENCES

Geraerts, E., M. M. Arnold, D. Stephen Lindsay, H. Merckelbach, M. Jelicic, and B. Hauer. 2006. Forgetting of prior remembering in persons reporting recovered memories of childhood sexual abuse. *Psychological Science* 17:1002–8.
Geraerts, E., E. Smeets, M. Jelicie, H. Merckelbach, and J. van Heerden. 2006. Retrieval inhibition of trauma-related words in women reporting repressed or recovered memories of childhood sexual abuse. *Behaviour Research and Therapy* 44: 1129–36.
Loftus, E. F. 2003. Make-believe memories. *American Psychologist* 58: 867–73.
McNally, R. J. 2003. *Remembering Trauma.* Cambridge, MA: Belknap Press/Harvard University Press.
Merckelbach, H., T. Smeeets, E. Geraerts, M. Jelicic, A. Bouwen, and E. Smeets. 2006. I haven't thought about this for years! Dating recent recalls of vivid memories. *Applied Cognitive Psychology* 20: 33–42.

29
Mental Ability: Use It or Lose It?

As people age, their scores on standard intelligence tests decrease. Also, with the exception of vocabulary size, other measures of mental functioning also decrease with age. The inverse relationship between various types of mental ability and age is pretty well established. In our competitive, can-do society, whenever we hear about some ability declining as we get older, we get upset and immediately ask, "How do I slow that process down?" One typical answer to that question stresses staying mentally active. The importance of mental activity is always brought out in those TV interviews with some local person who just turned 100 and is sharp as a tack.

> *Interviewer:* "How do you manage to stay so mentally sharp?"
> *Subject:* "I stay mentally active. I do crossword puzzles every day, and like to help my great-great grandson with his algebra homework. Keeps my brain in shape."

OK, maybe so. But there's always a problem with taking a link between two things and establishing which is causing which. For instance, studies show that healthy people are more sexually active. Does that mean having sex will keep one healthy, or does the link merely show that healthy people have the energy to engage in sex? The same issue relates to our 100-year-old; is it that doing crossword puzzles causes her brain to function better, or is the old gal mentally sharp to begin with, and that is why she can do the puzzles and other mental tasks?

QUESTION: *Will staying mentally active slow down my decline in mental ability as I age?*
RESEARCH ANSWER: *No.*

ANALYSIS

Tim Salthouse of the University of Virginia gives us a thorough review of studies that bear on this issue. He looks at a variety of research projects that put people in mental-training programs and then do follow-up mental measurements on them, sometimes several years later. Generally, the results have been disappointing. And when some positive results occur, they are open to alternative interpretations, or the time span between training and testing is not long enough to provide a valid test of the basic proposition. So the best we can say right now is: Evidence that engaging in mental activity will slow the decline of mental ability as we age is far from convincing.

So what should we do? Say the hell with it and stop "exercising our brains"? Absolutely not! A fundamental road to establishing good psychological health and well-being is to monitor our thinking and our behavior and always strive to control and improve both. We must willingly face challenges and confront obstacles with a can-do attitude, and resist tendencies toward apathy and laziness. Thus, we agree with Salthouse, who says:

> Although ... the mental-exercise hypothesis is more of an optimistic hope than an empirical reality, ... people should behave as though it were true. People should continue to engage in mentally stimulating activities because ... there is no evidence that it has any harmful effects, the activities are often enjoyable and may contribute to a higher quality of life. (Salthouse 1996)

As we age, there is always a danger of becoming discouraged as we see ourselves unable to do things as effectively or easily as we used to. Many activities, both physical and mental, become more challenging. Challenge, however, does not mean we should quit; challenge simply means we adjust our goals to be consistent with the realistic limits an aging body and brain impose on us. It is also important to remember that new learning can indeed take place in older people, although as Arthur Kramer and Sherry Willis point out, the new learning is often quite specific.

We probably need to stop being obsessed with longevity. We should not exercise, eat well, and avoid health-compromising habits like smoking or excessive alcohol consumption so we can live a long time. Rather, we should follow that type of lifestyle so that we feel pretty good physically and mentally the next morning.

PRIMARY REFERENCE

Salthouse, T. A. 2006. Mental exercise and mental aging. *Perspectives on Psychological Science* 1: 68–87.

ADDITIONAL REFERENCES

Hoyer, W. J., and P. Verhaeghen. 2006. Memory aging. In *Handbook of the Psychology of Aging, 6th ed.,* edited by J. E. Birren and K. W. Schaie (209–32). San Diego, CA: Elsevier.

Kramer, A. F., and S. L. Willis. 2002. Enhancing the cognitive vitality of older adults. *Current Directions in Psychological Science* 11: 173–77.

Rhodes, M. G., and C. M. Kelley. 2005. Executive processes, memory accuracy, and memory monitoring: An aging and individual difference analysis. *Journal of Memory and Language* 52: 578–94.

Salthouse, T. A. 1996. Processing-speed theory of adult age differences in cognition. *Psychological Review* 103: 403–28.

30
Is Intelligence a Factor in Longevity?

As we noted in the previous section, we're always looking for an edge to help us live longer. We know things like good diet, exercise, moderate alcohol consumption, and not smoking are good for us and, although not guaranteeing a long life, certainly increase our odds of longevity. Not too long ago there was also a research report that said sexual activity contributes to a long and healthy life. That's right, sex. Apparently, the researchers went into a village in Great Britain and asked the men there how often they had sex. Some years later they returned to the village and found that those who had sex more often were still alive, whereas the less sexually active men were either dead or not doing too well on the health front. Of course, when you think about it, these results really don't tell us that having sex will make us live longer. One way to interpret the results is to say those men who were having a lot of sex were doing so because they were already healthy and vigorous. Their good health and energy gave them the stamina to have sex and also contributed to their longer (and certainly more fun!) lives.

Good diet, exercise, not smoking—such habits will no doubt make us feel better when we're alive and kicking, and may even help us live longer. Here's a question for you, though: How about intelligence? Do smart people live longer? By "smart" we don't mean people who have the good sense to obey traffic signals and speed limits, to avoid deserted areas of town at 2 A.M., and to resist walking up to NFL-sized strangers and shout, "You lookin' for trouble, you ugly sonofabitch?" No way! By smart, we mean people who score high on intelligence tests, college-entrance exams, and other standardized tests of intellectual ability and achievement.

QUESTION: *Is intelligence as measured on standard test instruments associated with a longer life?*
RESEARCH ANSWER: *Yes.*

ANALYSIS

First, let's define the term *intelligence*. We're referring here to IQ (intelligence quotient) as measured on a standardized, valid, and reliable intelligence test, such the Wechsler Adult Intelligence Scale, the Stanford-Binet IQ test, or any one of a number of other intelligence measures recognized in the psychological profession.

Linda Gottfredson and Ian Deary describe the results of a long-term study in Scotland, where IQ scores of over 87,000 children born in 1921 were assessed in 1932. Decades later, various studies have looked at longevity rates in the sample and associated age at death with the childhood IQ scores. Obviously, records for all of the original population were not available, but the researchers were able to obtain samples of several thousand people. Here are some representative findings. Remember, when we refer to an IQ score, we are referring to that score measured when the subjects were 11 years old.

- A 15-point decrease in IQ (such as, those who had an IQ of 100 versus those who had an IQ of 85) meant that the person was only 79 percent as likely to reach age 76 as those with the higher IQ.

- For each 15-point decrease in IQ (such as, 130, 115, 100, 85) there was a 17 percent higher risk of dying compared to the higher IQ.

- The 15-point decrease in IQ was associated with a 27 percent increase in deaths due to cancer in men, and a 40 percent increase in women.

- Lower IQ scores were associated with higher rates of death due to coronary heart disease and lung cancer.

- For people age 50, IQ had a greater effect on death rates for those living in poorer areas compared to those living in affluent areas.

- IQ scores were not associated with the likelihood of beginning smoking as a young adult, but were associated with the likelihood of quitting smoking later in life.

Of course, a variety of factors could be playing a role in these relationships. For instance, higher IQ people may have higher-paying jobs and better financial resources, and be able to afford better health care. Also, those with a higher IQ may take better care of themselves. They might also be better equipped cognitively to understand the relationship between behavior and illness, and be better able to follow treatment regimens prescribed for sickness. Whatever the exact cause of the relationship between IQ and health and longevity, it is also possible that people with a higher IQ are more likely to engage in health-enhancing behaviors, and these behaviors contribute to a longer lifespan. (We're willing to bet, however, that you join us in knowing some pretty intelligent people who seem to ignore their physical health!)

Some might want to say that people who have a high IQ were born with a better functioning brain and also a better functioning body. Thus, in these people not only do their brain cells work at a very efficient capacity, but also their other body cells work very efficiently, thus keeping the person alive longer. We don't know of any biological test, however, that would verify this hypothesis. For the time being, therefore, it must remain a hypothesis.

Whatever the interpretation offered for the data we mentioned earlier, the extensive knowledge you show on this topic in or out of class will lead your friends and professors to predict you're in for a long life.

PRIMARY REFERENCE

Gottfredson, L. S., and I. J. Deary. 2004. Intelligence predicts health and longevity, but why? *Current Directions in Psychology* 13: 1–4.

ADDITIONAL REFERENCES

Gottfredson, L. S. 1997. Why *g* matters. The complexity of everyday life. *Intelligence* 24: 79–132.

Gottfredson, L. S. 1998. The general intelligence factor. *Scientific American Presents* 9: 24–29.

Gottfredson, L. S. 2004. Intelligence: Is it the epidemiologists' elusive "fundamental cause" of social class inequalities in health? *Journal of Personality and Social Psychology* 86: 174–99.

Hart, C. L., I. J. Deary, M. D. Taylor, P. L. MacKinnon, G. Davey Smith, L. J. Whalley, V. Wilsone, D. J. Holea, and J. M. Starr. 2003. The Scottish Mental Survey 1932 linked to the Midspan studies: A prospective investigation of childhood intelligence and future health. *Public Health* 117: 187–95.

31
Does Good Spelling Produce Good Communication?

Anyone who spends time sending text messages or dwelling in chat rooms knows there are a lot of shortcuts and abbreviations to avoid having to spell out a complete word. Purists among us cringe at this misuse of English, and even say we are rapidly reaching the point where spelling won't matter.

Actually, the threat to correct spelling in the instant communication age may be greater than we imagine. For instance, not too long ago, one of those joke messages popped up in one of our spam e-mails that was full of misspellings. This was one of those mass e-mails that instantly goes out to the entire world. The point of the message was simple: we can misspell words horribly, but as long the first and last letters are placed correctly, we can decipher the word even though the middle letters are jumbled. Researcher Jennifer Stover and colleagues share an example:

> Aoccdrnig to a rscheeracehr at Cmabrigde Uinervtisy, it deosn't mttaer wrehe the ltteers are, the iprmoetnt tnhig is I the frist and lsat ltteer be at the rghit pclae.

Cute, huh? Believe us, it's tough to type out that passage (and the sentence plays havoc with spellcheck!); we're so used to typing words correctly that our brain really doesn't like to direct our fingers to do otherwise. Well-practiced habits can be a great thing. And, in fact, one explanation why we are able to understand the above message is that our brain reads "whole" words and does not simply assemble individual letters into a meaningful whole. If that's the case, then the hell with spelling, right? Just get the letters in their (Oops! We mean "there," of course!) somehow, and make sure the first and last letters are correct; our brains will do the rest.

QUESTION: *Is correct spelling needed for us to be able to read written material efficiently?*
RESEARCH ANSWER: *Yes.*

ANALYSIS

Are you surprised at the answer? After all, you had no problem reading that passage above, did you? We confess we cheated a bit in phrasing our question by adding that key word, "efficiently." Yes, you were able to read that above passage OK, but actually you may have had more trouble than you realized. Stover and colleagues considered this possibility. The researchers prepared written materials, with words correctly or incorrectly spelled. They controlled for reading ability among their participants and length of the material, and used paragraphs that were either simple or complex in content. All participants were timed for how long it took to read the material. Also, after reading the material, they tested the participants for comprehension of the material. The researchers also asked how comfortable and frustrated their participants felt while reading and how well they thought they comprehended the material.

The results showed that it took longer to read the scrambled material, especially when it was complex in nature. The participants also reported they were less comfortable and more frustrated while reading the scrambled material compared to when reading the normal material. Furthermore, these effects increased for the complex material.

The only measure that showed no difference between the scrambled and unscrambled passages was comprehension. The comprehension, however, came at a price: time and comfort level. Thus, the spam e-mail claim that correct spelling doesn't matter is bogus. Imagine that! Bogus spam e-mail. What are the odds?

So all you lusoy sleplres out there who tuohhgt you had an ecsxue and cluod oreolvok a wsakeens in slelpnig, freogt it! Lraen how to slepl!!

PRIMARY REFERENCE

Stover, J., T. Dismuke, C. Nelson, and J. E. Grahe. 2006. Can you raed this srcmabeld msesgae? Testing a mass e-mail assertion. *Psi Chi Journal of Undergraduate Research* 11: 77–83.

ADDITIONAL REFERENCES

Balota, D., M. Cortese, S. Sergent-Marshall, D. Spieler, and M. Yap. 2004. Visual word recognition of single-syllable words. *Journal of experimental Psychology* 133: 283–316.

Jordan, J., S. Thomas, G. Patching, and K. Scott-Brown. 2003. Assessing the importance of letter pairs in initial, exterior, and interior positions in reading. *Journal of Experimental Psychology: Learning, Memory, and Cognition* 29: 883–93.

Kwantes, P., and D. Mewhor. 1999. Evidence for sequential processing in visual word recognition. *Journal of Experimental Psychology Human Perception and Performance* 25: 376–81.

Witte, K., and J. Freund. 2001. Single-letter retrieval cues for anagram solution. *Journal of General Psychology* 128: 315–28.

32
How Soon Do Speakers Lose Their Audiences?

Think back to a time when you were listening to someone give a speech. Maybe the occasion was a training session for a summer job or an internship; maybe it was listening to a guest speaker who came into your classroom; maybe it was a politician who came to talk at your school. Whatever the situation, reflect for a

minute on how the speaker held your attention. When many people make such a reflection they say something like this:

> I was very interested in hearing this speaker and what she [or he] had to say. I remember eagerly following the talk carefully at first. After about 10 minutes, though, my attention began to wander. I found myself looking at other people in the room, or thinking about what I still had to do after the meeting, or wondering why the speaker happened to choose that particular clothing color. Whatever was going through my mind, it was clear I had lost some of the focused attention on what was being said that I had at the beginning of the speech.

We are college professors. It is almost an accepted law in the profession that whereas we may have your undivided attention at the beginning of class, after about 15 minutes we have lost you; you've gone to another planet, an alternate universe, a different level of consciousness! Oh, yeh, you're sitting there, eyes open, pen in hand, maybe even looking at us at the front of the room. Your glazed eyes betray you, however, and tell us you are not processing the class topic, are thinking of how you're going to find time to study for a test, or find ways to get lucky this weekend.

Speakers and presenters are also keenly aware of this accepted audience law, and also look for ways to overcome the "15-minute limit of audience attention" principle. Such strategies usually involve things like using vivid audiovisual props, calling on members of the audience, engaging the audience in interactive exercises, or knocking them dead with humor mixed into the formal talk.

QUESTION: *Is the "15-minute limit of audience attention" principle based on solid research?*

RESEARCH ANSWER: *No.*

ANALYSIS

Karen Wilson and James Korn of Saint Louis University decided to take a look at the research on the 15-minute principle. Although they restricted their analysis to research to college students in class, we believe what they have to say is also relevant to any situation involving a formal speaker delivering a message to an audience. In a nutshell, Wilson and Korn say there is little support for the 15-minute principle. A few of the results they report are as follows:

- Student note-taking is fairly stable throughout a standard class period.

- Some studies report making observations of students during a class and report behavioral signs of reduced attention (such as yawning, eyes closed, fidgeting, whispering to a neighbor) as the class proceeded. Generally, however, these studies can be criticized as lacking valid and reliable measurement techniques, and also showing great variability from student to student and teacher to teacher.

- There is usually no difference in student retention of material from the beginning, middle, and end of the class. Some studies indicate excellent learning of material in the last 20 minutes of the class.

- In one study, student self-reports of concentration levels during a class showed maximum concentration at the beginning of the session. There was, however, large variation in this finding across different professors. One might expect a similar large variation across different students, but this variability was not reported.

If you are faced with speaking before an audience, say giving a long in-class presentation or a speech, it would appear there is no need for you to assume, "I will have the audience for the first few minutes, and after that I may have to struggle." Going before an audience with that sort of preconception is probably going to work against you because the audience will sense you're treating them like a bunch of inattentive ignoramuses. In that case, they will not like you! By the same token, accepting the 15-minute principle may lead you to overlook the quality of your opening remarks and concentrate on the later stuff. In that case, you may lose your audience in the first minute because you're boring and disorganized right out of the gate. Any sort of presentation, of course, whether spoken or written, can profit by providing a hook, a "gotcha," to capture the audience right at the beginning. After that, just keep the presentation lively, varied in tone and style, and with opportunities for audience participation.

We suspect that the 15-minute principle kicks in when presentations are somewhat monotonous in voice tone, lacking props and audiovisual aids, somber, and fact-based. Think of the stereotypical old professor shuffling into class, standing behind the podium, opening a notes folder, announcing "Today our topic is the Normandy invasion," lecturing in a monotone for 50 minutes, closing the notes folder, and then shuffling out of the room. (WAKE UP! We probably just put you to sleep with that description.) We might as well ask you to concentrate on a spot on the wall for 50 minutes!

This whole discussion reminds us of the visit to our campus several years by then-president of the United States, Bill Clinton. He spoke in a crowded, very hot and stuffy gymnasium for well over 30 minutes. We remember how the opening 5 to 10 minutes were incredibly boring. There were the usual thanks and recognitions of dignitaries on the stage, and then some platitudes and fancy campaign-style phrases.

The only thing that held the audience attention for those 10 minutes was the fact that they were looking live at a sitting president of the United States. Anyone else and they would have begun filing out of the uncomfortable gym. And then a remarkable thing happened, a reverse 15-minute principle, if you will. Slowly, almost unnoticed, President Clinton began to deviate from his notes and speak to young college students. His voice rose and his conviction appeared to strengthen. He spoke with them, not to them; he touched on issues vital to their lives; we bet that nearly every student in that crowded auditorium felt he was speaking directly and personally to them. Even a Republican was awestruck at his masterful ability to transfix and capture an audience.

Tell your friends that the 15-minute principle is an excuse! It's an excuse offered up by an unprepared inefficient presenter or lecturer; it's also an excuse offered up by tired, lazy, apathetic audience members who see no need to be present.

PRIMARY REFERENCE
Wilson, K., and J. H. Korn. 2007. Attention during lectures: Beyond ten minutes. *Teaching of Psychology* 34: 85–89.

ADDITIONAL REFERENCES
Benjamin, L. T., Jr. 2002. Lecturing. In *The Teaching of Psychology: Essays in Honor of Wilbert J. McKeachie and Charles L. Brewer,* edited by S. F. Davis and W. Buskist (57–67). Mahwah, NJ: Erlbaum.

Goss Lucas, S., and D. A. Bernstein. 2005. *Teaching Psychology: A Step by Step Guide.* Mahwah, NJ: Erlbaum.

McKeachie, W. J., and M. Svinicki. 2006. *McKeachie's Teaching Tips: Strategies, Research, and Theory for College and University Teachers,* 12th edition, Boston: Houghton-Mifflin.

Wankat, P. C. 2002. *The Effective, Efficient Professor: Teaching, Scholarship and Service.* Boston: Allyn and Bacon.

PART FIVE

ANXIETY, STRESS, AND STAYING COOL

33
Are Smoking and Panic Attacks Related?

Smoking cigarettes is currently a great evil in American society. It is becoming more and more difficult for someone to find a place to light-up legally, and without angry and aggressive looks from others nearby. Moreover, who can deny the ravaging effects of smoking on our bodies? Indeed, many view this health-compromising behavior as akin to slow and methodical suicide.

But we're talking psychology here, and in this section we consider panic attacks. How many people do you know who say they have suffered panic attacks? Many people take antianxiety medication to help them avoid such attacks. If these sufferers also smoke, perhaps they should consider quitting, which brings us to our question.

QUESTION: *Is cigarette smoking a risk factor for panic attacks?*
RESEARCH ANSWER: *Yes.*

ANALYSIS

Michael Zvolensky and Amit Bernstein of the University of Vermont reviewed literature bearing on this topic. They note that 40 percent of those seeking treatment for panic disorder are current smokers, compared to 19 percent of those who are extremely shy in social situations, and 22 percent of those with obsessive-compulsive disorder.

Let's note that the 40 percent figure reported above means that 60 percent of panic sufferers are NOT smokers. Still, the relationship between smoking and panic disorder is there and is a two-way street. The two conditions often (not always) occur together: smoking may help instigate and maintain panic attacks, and the panic condition probably also contributes to the smoking.

It's not too hard to imagine some of the factors that may be involved in this relationship. Maybe for some people the physical effects of smoking (heart palpitations and feeling anxious, for instance) contribute to feelings of panic. Maybe some people are somewhat naturally anxious because of an overactive nervous system, and that characteristic makes them good candidates for both panic attacks and smoking. Many smokers also seem to be in a perpetual state of trying to quit; perhaps nicotine withdrawal symptoms in these individuals contribute to panic attacks.

All of these possible causes and relationships are found in the literature. The relationship between panic and smoking is complex and varies from person to person. But whatever the particular cause for a specific individual, the link is there, and smokers can add another negative (panic attacks) to the list of why quitting is a good idea. Of course if you mention all this stuff to a smoker you'll probably get a cigarette put out on your forehead!

PRIMARY REFERENCE
Zvolensky, M. J., and A. Bernstein. 2005. Cigarette smoking and panic psychopathology. *Current Directions in Psychological Science* 14: 301–5.

ADDITIONAL REFERENCES
Breslau, N., and D. F. Klein. 1999. Smoking and panic attacks: An epidemiologic investigation. *Archives of General Psychiatry* 56: 1141–47.
Goodwin, R., and S. P. Hamilton. 2002. Cigarette smoking and panic: The role of neuroticism. *American Journal of Psychiatry* 159: 1208–13.

Lasser, K., J. W. Boyd, S. Woolhandler, D. U. Himmelstein, D. McCormick, and D. H. Bor. 2000. Smoking and mental illness: A population-based prevalence study. *JAMA: Journal of the American Medical Association* 284: 2606–10.

McCabe, R. E., S. M. Chudzik, M. M. Antony, L. Young, R. P. Sinson, and M. J. Zvolensky. 2004. Smoking behaviors across anxiety disorders. *Journal of Anxiety Disorders* 18: 7–18.

Zvolensky, M. J., M. T. Feldner, E. W. Leen-Feldner, and A. McLeish. 2005. Smoking and panic attacks, panic disorder, and agoraphobia: A review of the empirical literature. *Clinical Psychology Review* 25: 761–89.

34
Does Lashing Out at Others Help?

Are you angry? Really pissed off? Well, get it off your chest; let it out. Give the source of your anger a good yell or scolding; let them know what you really think about them. Write a nasty letter or give them a phone call. Pound a pillow, throw a bottle against a brick wall—do SOMETHING to get that anger out. You'll feel better afterwards. Or will you?

During class discussion on topics concerning aggression, emotion, motivation, and similar topics, students invariably answer particular questions with the "catharsis" explanation: "People often do things to 'get their frustrations out' because they know that releasing what's bothering them will calm them down."

This catharsis, or energy-release idea, is very pervasive in students' thinking about human behavior and treats us like overinflated balloons ready to pop unless some pressure is released. The notion of energy release as a safety valve is very intuitive and seems to make good common sense. The fact is, however, formal evidence supporting it is lacking.

QUESTION: *Does vigorous expression of anger help get it out of your system?*
RESEARCH ANSWER: *No.*

ANALYSIS

A number of studies have been set up to frustrate and anger participants. For instance, imagine volunteering for an experiment that requires you to work with a partner who is a fumbling idiot (actually a confederate of the experimenter whose purpose is to make your life miserable). What happens in this and similar situations is that you get quite aggravated and your blood pressure shoots up; you are more likely to ventilate your anger by not cooperating with others and even taking steps to undermine others' efforts. If you are allowed to express some aggression toward others in the experiment, you will be more likely to repeat that aggression compared to participants who were allowed to let their anger subside. In other words, expressing anger seems to increase the likelihood of later anger displays, not decrease them. Venting does not reduce later episodes of aggression.

The problem with venting anger and "getting it off my chest" with aggressive displays is that you are teaching yourself to resolve conflicts and frustration in aggressive, as opposed to constructive, ways. When people practice more assertive and cooperative ways of expressing anger, they feel better and calmer. When they practice aggressive ways of expressing anger, they feel worse, agitated, and still angry. If you have been taught that it is good to let emotions out, express your frustrations and anger, and get things off your chest, you are not being taught to manage, control, and direct emotions in socially appropriate ways. Rather, you are being taught to lash out at others when things don't go your way. In this case, venting will not make you feel better; you will simply learn an abusive and aggressive habit.

This topic is an excellent one to research and should generate a lot of class discussion because the conclusions go against everyday common sense and advice to "let it all out." This advice is based on short-term results. That is, yelling at someone because of pent-up anger you have been holding in may indeed give you temporary relief. That relief is rewarding, and the response that has been re-inforced is "yelling," or putting someone "down." A basic principle from Psychology 101 is that rewards increase the likelihood of behavior that produces the reward. Thus, in this case, you are simply teaching yourself to become a person who yells at others who frustrate you. This behavior pattern, of course, will not serve you well in your long-term social interactions.

PRIMARY REFERENCE

Bushman, B. J., et al. 2005. Chewing on it can chew you up: Effects of rumination on trig-gered displaced aggression. *Journal of Personality and Social Psychology* 88: 1027–40.

ADDITIONAL REFERENCES

Bushman, B. J. 2002. Does venting anger feed or extinguish the flame? Catharsis, rumina-tion, distraction, anger, and aggressive responding. *Personality and Social Psychology Bulletin* 28: 724–31.

Bushman, B. J., and C. A. Anderson. 2001. Is it time to pull the plug on the hostile versus instrumental aggression dichotomy? *Psychological Review* 108: 273–79.

De Castro, B. O., J. W. Veerman, W. Koops, J. D. Bosch, and H. J. Monshouwer. 2002. Hos-tile attribution of intent and aggressive behavior: A meta-analysis. *Child Develop-ment* 73: 1467–86.

Vasquez, E. A., T. F. Denson, W. C. Pedersen, D. M. Strenstrom, and N. Miller. 2005. The moderating effect of trigger intensity on triggered displaced aggression. *Journal of Experimental Social Psychology* 41: 61–67.

35

Should We Hide Our Weaknesses from Others?

Imagine yourself in a job interview.

> *Interviewer:* "Now this job will require you to stand in front an audience from time to time and speak to them for about 30 minutes. Does that present any problems?"

Before we suggest two possible answers, let's establish that you REALLY DO suffer some anxiety when you get up in front of an audience. We don't mean you faint or tremble uncontrollably and have to run out of the room; we simply mean you get nervous, self-conscious, and would prefer not to speak in front of people unless absolutely necessary. OK, with those characteristics in mind, let's go back and give two possible replies to the interviewer's question above.

> *Reply A:* "Funny you should ask that. Truth is, I do get a little nervous and anxious when I'm speaking in front of a group. Because of that tend-ency, I do a lot of thorough preparation before a presentation. I practice and rehearse extensively what I'm going to say. When I really prepare,

I find I'm less likely to stutter or forget my train of thought. So as long as I know in advance about having to give a presentation, my answer is no, that requirement of the job does not present a problem."
Reply B: "No, that requirement of the job does not present a problem."

Many factors, of course, most of which are out of our control, go into determining the outcome of a job interview. However, the two options above raise a fundamental question about how much we should divulge about ourselves in such a situation. In Reply A, for instance, a susceptibility to anxiety is made quite clear, although at the same time, the response makes note of successful attempts to deal with it. Reply B, on the other hand, implies complete confidence and control when faced with a public presentation, which is less than truthful.

As we pose our research question, let's note that we do not intend to limit the question to a job interview. In fact, the research we will discuss deals with a variety of situations in which one acknowledges weaknesses in social situations. What we're interested in is the effect such admission has on the other person; that is, whether the other person perceives us more or less favorably when we admit to some weakness.

QUESTION: *In a social interaction, if we admit to some negative trait or characteristic, will others judge us more positively?*
RESEARCH ANSWER: *Yes.*

ANALYSIS

Andres Ward and Lyle Brenner of Swarthmore College and the University of Florida developed some situations for their research participants. In the first situation, college students had to read a paragraph and rate it according to its clarity. For one group of students, the material was *preceded* by a statement that the paragraph was confusing. For two other groups, an identical statement either came *after* the paragraph or was *never given*. The results showed that the first group (confusing statement preceding the reading) rated the paragraph as clearer than did the other two groups.

In the second situation, students listened to a taped lecture by a speaker with a heavy Austrian accent. For half the students, the lecture was preceded by the speaker's statement of having a strong accent; no such statement occurred for the other half of the listeners. The results showed that the students who heard the "I have a strong accent" statement rated the speaker as clearer, more likeable, and having more years of speaking English, than did the students who did not hear the statement admitting to a strong accent.

In the third situation, students evaluated the application of a hypothetical college applicant. For one group of evaluators, the application included a statement from both the student and his or her guidance counselor that the applicant's grades were not really the greatest. For the rest of the evaluators, no such statements occurred in the application materials. The results showed that the evaluators who had the "not the greatest grades" statement included rated the grades more favorably for admission than did the evaluators who did not have such a negative admission from the applicant.

One thing is very important to note in these studies: Admission of a negative quality pertaining to some ability led to more positive evaluations of the individual being described, but the positive evaluation was *specific to that ability*. For instance, in the last scenario, whereas grades were judged more favorably when the applicant admitted they weren't the best, SAT scores were not rated more favorably. Thus, global impressions of a person are not necessarily influenced when that person admits to a specific vulnerability in a specific area. But there's a clear lesson in all this discussion: a little dose of humility can go a long way, and it never hurts to bring yourself down a level or two, especially if you are being presented as somewhat of an expert. Let's consider a hypothetical situation.

Your father's boss assigns him a project evaluating strategies and performance outcomes in a particular division of his company. Dad spends weeks and weeks at this task, studying statistics and strategic plans, interviewing employees at all levels, and making comparisons with statistical models. After six months he completes a comprehensive, thorough, and instructive presentation outlining all aspects of the project, including recommendations for implementation in other divisions of the company.

The boss schedules his presentation before all the employees in a large lecture hall. Your dad is introduced as an expert on the issues under discussion because he has lived with and studied these issues for the past several months. That's nice, but all Dad wants is for his fellow employees to "buy into" his message, even though some of those messages may mean more work for them, or the need to learn new skills.

According to Ward and Brenner, Dad would do well to sprinkle his presentation with some negative comments about himself. By negative we mean a few well-placed, not overdone, humbling and self-effacing comments, which should go a long way in making him more likeable to his audience.

> Thanks, Mr. Brown. You make me sound like some kind of expert here, but the truth of the matter is I feel I've been stumbling around some pretty complex issues and running into a lot of blind alleys. What I'm going to present today is really a work in progress, and I hope some observations from the audience can help point us in fruitful directions. Lord knows I need the help in working toward a useful plan for us.

To increase the likelihood that the audience accepts the clarity of his presentation, it might also help if Dad admitted some negative characteristics of his method of presentation as he goes along:

> I really struggled over this graph here, and it just may not be the best way to present the data. I hope I can hit the main points here.

Finally, when he gets to the recommendations, a little honesty never hurts:

> Now if you'll allow me to indulge in some admittedly over-generalized, over-simplified conclusions, I'd like to make some broad proposals.

Obviously, Dad still may go down in flames. Acknowledging negative aspects carries risks. The point of this discussion, however, is simply that we too often go out of our way to avoid any mention of negativity about ourselves. We wear personality armor to shield our shortcomings, lest we be judged negatively. A much better approach, however, is to acknowledge some shortcomings, display some genuine humility, and show ourselves to be quite human.

Remember, listeners have their own personal doubts and weaknesses. If we show some of our own, we become more like them in their eyes, and more likeable.

PRIMARY REFERENCE

Ward, A., and L. Brenner. 2006. Accentuate the negative: The positive effects of negative acknowledgment. *Psychological Science* 17: 959–62.

ADDITIONAL REFERENCES

Brown, P., and S. C. Levinson. 1987. *Politeness: Some Universals in Language.* Cambridge, England: Cambridge University Press.

Gibson, B., and D. Sachau. 2000. Sandbagging as a self-presentational strategy: Claiming to be less than you are. *Personality and Social Psychology Bulletin* 26: 56–70.

Hastorf, A. H., J. Wildfogel, and T. Cassman. 1979. Acknowledgment of handicap as a tactic in social interaction. *Journal of Personality and Social Psychology* 37: 1790–97.

Tice, D. M., J. L. Butler, M. B. Muraven, and A. M. Stillwell. 1995. When modesty prevails: Differential favorability of self-presentation to friends and strangers. *Journal of Personality and Social Psychology* 69: 1120–38.

36
Is Optimism Good for Your Health?

We all know people who see the cup as half-empty and others who see it as half-full. Optimists and pessimists, right? We label others and ourselves as one type or the other in most situations. If we had our choice about things, we would probably like ourselves to be optimists. But be careful about that, some say; it's dangerous to tempt fate. If we say things are going to go smoothly, we know the gods are ready to pounce on us and mess everything up. At least that's the way some of us think when it comes to sharing our successes with others.

One thing is for sure: Do we want to hang around with a pessimist, a grouch, the one who brings us down by always looking on the dark side of things? A pessimistic spouse is a threat to marital stability; a pessimistic work colleague is a threat to productivity and morale; a pessimistic friend is ... well, a soon-to-be-former friend.

Some say being a pessimist is an appropriate way to view reality. To a pessimist, the optimist is unrealistic. For instance, a couple may have plans for a golf outing. One says, "Did you hear the weather forecast? And look at those clouds. Our golf round is going to be ruined. What a bummer. I hate rain."

Well, there's no doubt that the expectation of rain mirrors what may be shaping up as reality, but the optimist might point out: "Yep, looks bad. We better put the golf clubs away. Remember that movie we've been wanting to watch? Let's make some popcorn and hot chocolate and have a snuggly movie afternoon."

The pessimist's retort? "But the forecast calls for bad thunderstorms, heavy winds, and possible downed power lines. Why get involved in a movie and then have the power go out?"

"Screw it then," responds the optimistic mate. "I'm going drinking with the guys."

Realism is not the issue here; the issue is how you respond to reality. If you're a downer, you'll find yourself in conflict with others, and eventually alone. Your emotional approach to life, therefore, will certainly influence your social network and the number of supportive friends you have. How do you explain your life circumstances? We all experience failure in our lives; we all have setbacks; we are all rejected at times by others. How do you interpret these events *in general*? Are you to blame? Sometimes you are. But if self-blame is your habitual pattern of approaching setbacks, you're setting yourself up for future problems.

How do you react to a job interview? If you have prepared for the interview and see it as a chance to show someone the skills and qualities that will make you a desirable employee, you are viewing the interview as a challenge you can meet successfully. Your preparation and optimistic frame of mind put you in a relaxed and confident state that will make you appear to be a desirable candidate. The odds are you will have a successful interview. But if you view the interview as threatening, as something that will expose your weaknesses and shortcomings, your pessimistic outlook will almost guarantee that what you fear will happen.

Your pessimistic demeanor will make you more defensive, less likeable, and a less desirable candidate to the interviewer, and the interview will be just what you thought—a disaster.

Our emotional states have much to do with how we get along with other people, but what about our physical health? Can an optimistic approach to life translate into good physical health? Does pessimism increase our odds of getting sick?

QUESTION: *Do positive and negative emotional states affect our physical health?*
RESEARCH ANSWER: *Yes.*

ANALYSIS

Sheldon Cohen and Sarah Pressman of Carnegie Mellon University talk about the concept of positive affect. This phrase refers to a set of emotions and feelings that bring pleasure, enjoyment, and satisfaction in one's general approach to life. The researchers note that when it comes to physical health, most discussion in psychology centers around negative emotional states like anxiety and depression, and the devastating effects these states can have on us. Positive affect, they say, has been somewhat ignored, especially the role of positive emotional states on our physical health.

In a typical study from Cohen's laboratory, participants are assessed with respect to their level of positive affect versus negative affect. Those high in positive affect tend to be lively, energetic, cheerful, and relaxed; those high in negative affect tend to be sad, nervous, and short-tempered. After assessment over several weeks, the participants are then exposed to cold viruses and monitored closely over the next few days. In one study, those high in positive affect were less likely to catch a cold than those high in negative affect.

Other studies find similar results when looking at other health conditions. One study looked at immune system functioning in first-year law school students two months after the school year began. Students who had been categorized as optimists showed significantly better immune system functioning than did students who had been categorized as pessimists. Optimism has also been found to raise the number of infection-fighting killer cells in the immune system. Positive affect has also been linked to lower rates of stroke and cardiovascular problems.

Is an optimistic attitude a guarantee of a long and healthy life? Of course not, no more than are eating a healthy diet, exercising, and not smoking guarantees of a long and healthy life. Whereas a positive outlook can bolster our immune system, there is little evidence that such an outlook can cure us from an already contracted disease. There are studies, for instance, showing that survival time for terminal cancer patients is not affected by whether the patient is an optimist or a pessimist. (We consider this issue for the case of breast cancer in another entry.) We might ask, however, during the time one has left, whose quality of life is likely to be more tolerable—the optimist's or the pessimist's?

We believe it pays to be an optimist. Both physically and psychologically, realistic optimism is a health-enhancing behavior. Optimists are more likely to succeed and develop a "can-do" attitude about life's obstacles, characteristics that will trigger their immune systems to be stronger. For optimists, stress is not all it's cracked up to be! An optimistic outlook and having positive emotional states at our side are obviously great psychological support systems. And, we should always remember that we can learn to cultivate such tendencies in ourselves. We can learn to think about events in our lives more accurately, objectively, realistically, and rationally. In short, we can learn to confront adversity in more positive ways.

Many of us often casually say, "I'm too much of a pessimist; I need to be more of an optimist." A comment like this one is not always valid and can cause us to underestimate ourselves. For instance, one of our students made precisely this comment at the end of a summer course. The students were asked to reflect on what they had learned in the course and what, if anything, the material had taught them about themselves. One student was going through the "I'm too pessimistic" speech, and really putting himself down for not being more optimistic about his life. We took issue with his self-disparaging comments and offered the following response:

> You say you're a pessimist, but consider the fact that you took this course during the summer. That behavior, that action, is a very optimistic choice. You chose to take on extra responsibility during summer vacation; you took a risk when you signed up for the course; you faced a challenge and took it on squarely. If that's not optimistic behavior, we don't know what is!

The message behind this reply is clear: *Before you decide your level of pessimism about life and yourself, take a good long look at your behavior, not at your casual spoken comments.* Talk is cheap. Behavior is where your essence lies.

There's another way that a pessimistic view of life can affect our health adversely. Some of us tend to believe that if an illness "runs in the family," we are doomed to get it. We all know people (not many, thank goodness) who have a tendency to explain some trait or characteristic they have by saying, "Well, it runs in the family." Whether the issue is cancer, heart problems, depression, anxiety, or insomnia, a type of surrender is suggested by these people when they sigh, "It's no use; the condition runs in the family. I'm going to get it."

QUESTION: *Do genetic risks mean our fate is sealed?*
RESEARCH ANSWER: *No.*

ANALYSIS

Many people are aware of the tendency for certain medical problems to be prevalent in their family. Because of that fact, they are careful to have early and thorough medical examinations, with a focus on particular problem areas. Some people extend this genetic vigilance into the psychological area. That is, they seek to explain certain psychological states as resulting from a genetic influence. "Come to think of it, Mom, Uncle Joe, and Grandma were always kind of miserable and depressed. Guess I got the gene. I'm doomed!"

We believe it is extremely dangerous to believe that because emotional or physical conditions "run in your family," you are destined to be a victim. Vigilance is wise, of course, especially where certain physical conditions can be diagnosed and corrected early, but we must always remember that a genetic risk does not mean we will inevitably be affected.

To illustrate the danger of this kind of thinking, consider the case of Mickey Mantle, the Hall of Fame baseball player who played with the New York Yankees in the 1950s and 1960s. As he aged into his late 50s, he often said, "If I knew I was going to live this long, I would have taken better care of myself." (This often quoted comment from Mantle is a favorite among the elderly.) Psychologist Janice Hastrup of the University of Buffalo puts the quote in a different context, however. Mickey Mantle had a family history of early death among the men in his family tree. His father died at 40 of Hodgkin's disease; he had some uncles who also never made it into their 50s. Anecdotal reports of those close to Mantle say he always believed he would be checking out of life early and, therefore, believed he might as well "live for today." So he lived according to the old hedonistic philosophy of "eat, drink, and be merry, for tomorrow we may die." Mantle especially focused on the "drink" part of that philosophy.

In an interview with Eric Jaffe of the Association for Psychological Science, Hastrup says that Mantle made the biggest error of his life, and one many of us make, by focusing excessively on a genetic vulnerability to cancer he believed he must have inherited. He felt early death was inevitable because of his inheritance, so he lived life somewhat recklessly, a lifestyle that turned into somewhat of a self-fulfilling prophecy. Yes, Mantle lived to the age of 63, an eternity for many Mantle males, but quite young for American men in the 1990s. Mantle's liver, however, was damaged by years of chronic alcoholism, cirrhosis, and hepatitis C. He developed liver cancer and had a transplant in June 1995. The liver cancer had spread, however, and Mantle died two months later.

Country music star Tim McGraw had a recent hit that also sums up this reaction to the inevitability of death: he went "sky diving, rocky mountain climbing, and rode 2.7 seconds on a bull name Fu-Manchu." In other words, if you think the end is near, grab life by the cojones and live on the edge.

Hastrup believes the faulty reasoning shown in the Mantle case leads people to believe they are helpless in the face of a genetic certainty; they believe there is nothing they can do to prevent the inevitable. This belief increases the likelihood they will engage in health-compromising behaviors as opposed to health-enhancing ones.

Hastrup, of course, is putting things in the context of a physical disease, but we believe the argument can be extended to emotional or psychological characteristics. We should not fall victim to a belief that because of a family history of some psychological state or characteristic, we, too, are certain to die young, or live a life victimized by things like shyness, unhappiness, depression, or anxiety.

Rather than succumb to the inevitable, awareness of a possible genetic vulnerability should serve to mobilize our health vigilance and encourage us to take a more active, assertive role in how we live life in general. Exercise, diet, frequent medical checkups, an optimistic attitude, medication—these things can help us take better control of our lives and walk through each day with more confidence, assertiveness, enjoyment, satisfaction, and happiness.

There's also a flip side to Hastrup's argument. You may be led into a false sense of security when your family history is one of longevity and resistance to certain diseases. If you believe you are somewhat invulnerable, you are more likely to lose focus on those lifestyles that you can control and that can increase your enjoyment of life. Do not get hung up on your family history. Concentrate on what you can control. *And there are only two things you can directly control: your thoughts and behavior.* Take charge of how you look at yourself and at the world around you. Choose appropriate and constructive actions, and you can have a very positive effect on the satisfaction you feel in living your life. If you decide to do further research on the topic of attitude and health, we think it is important to convey these messages.

PRIMARY REFERENCES

Cohen, S., and S. D. Pressman. 2006. Positive affect and health. *Current Directions in Psychological Science* 15: 122–25.

Jaffe, E. 2004. Mickey Mantle's greatest error. *American Psychological Society Observer* 17: 37.

ADDITIONAL REFERENCES

Cohen, S., W. J. Doyle, R. B. Turner, C. M. Alper, and D. P. Skoner. 2003. Emotional style and susceptibility to the common cold. *Psychosomatic Medicine* 65: 652–57.

Lyubominsky, S., L. King, and E. Diener. 2005. The benefits of frequent positive affect: Does happiness lead to success? *Psychological Bulletin* 131: 803–55.

Ostir, G. V., K. S. Markides, M. K. Peek, and J. S. Goodwin. 2001. The association between emotional well-being and the incidence of stroke in older adults. *Psychosomatic Medicine* 63: 210–15.

Pressman, S. D., and S. Cohen. 2005. Does positive affect influence health? *Psychological Bulletin* 131: 925–71.

Salovey, P., A. J. Rothman, J. B. Detweiler, and W. T. Seward. 2000. Emotional states and physical health. *American Psychologist* 55: 110–21.

37
Are Pets Good for Our Health?

"Life begins when the kids leave home and the dog dies." We don't know who uttered that phrase that gives all parents of teenagers and owners of kidney-challenged pets hope for the future, but it certainly seems to fly in the face of positive aspects of pet ownership (we won't try and mention any positive effects of managing teenagers!). Consider a dog. When it's young and rambunctious, every morning when you leave for the day, you might have to lock it in a crate that the CIA would consider an excellent torture chamber. Eight hours later you return and there is your loyal companion, lunging at the bars separating the two of you, unable to wait for you to unlock the door so it can leap into your arms, loving and forgiving and in no way blaming you for the agony you have inflicted. Talk about unconditional love!

No doubt you have read reports about the wonderful effect pets have on owners. In fact, you may even be familiar with programs that send a pooch to a local nursing home on a regular basis because its presence, even if only for a couple of hours, seems to have such a positive effect on the mood of the residents. Many of these types of anecdotal reports have been verified in research. Elderly folks who have pets, for instance, appear to make fewer physician visits; pet owners show better survival rates following heart attacks; and the presence of pets lowers blood pressure and other measures of cardiac stress.

All these findings are interesting and seem to establish a link between pet ownership and good health. Psychologists, however, are always wary of links, because a link does not establish which part of the link is having an influence on the other. This wariness is summed up in a statement you will hear whenever you take a course in introductory psychology: "Correlation does not mean causation." Karen Allen and her colleagues at the State University of New York at Buffalo, however, have performed an interesting and convincing study that seems to establish that it is the pets that cause the health benefits, and not simply that healthier people are more likely to take on the responsibility of pet ownership.

Allen and her colleagues took stockbrokers who were willing to adopt a pet as their study population, but randomly selected only half the group to adopt a dog or cat for the duration of the study. All the participants in the study had high blood pressure (at least 160/100). The results of the study showed that adopting a pet had a clear positive effect when the brokers were under stress; their blood pressure increase was less than half that of the brokers who had no pet.

Pets can be great, but how do they stack up against friends? We can't call the pet on the phone when we need someone to talk to; pets can't offer us advice on which course of action to take; they can't encourage us to keep going when the odds seem to be against us.

QUESTION: *Is the presence of friends more helpful in keeping blood pressure down in women than the presence of pets?*
RESEARCH ANSWER: *No.*

ANALYSIS

Animal haters just tossed this book into the trash! "Pets better than friends, members of our own species, people who know us and comfort us? No way!" Trust us, we're not putting friends down. First, note that our question is restricted to measuring blood pressure in women. Second, as we'll see in a minute, the question refers to a very specific context, women doing math problems in their head. Here's the setup. The same Karen Allen referred to earlier had participants perform some mental calculations under one of three conditions: alone, in the presence of a female friend, or in the presence of their dog. Compared to blood pressure in the alone condition, when the friends were present our math calculators showed an increase in blood pressure when doing the task; when the dog was present there was no such increase.

In a follow-up study, Allen and her colleagues used the same procedure, but this time they pitted the dog against a spouse-present condition. In the study, when men and women worked on math problems in the presence of their spouse, their blood pressure went from 120/80 to 155/100. However, when they worked in the presence of their pet, the math task took blood pressure to an average of only 125/83. (This result opens the door for many marriage jokes, but we'll just leave them up to you. Save them for the next family gathering.)

The math studies are interesting and lend themselves to a variety of interpretations. One simple explanation is that we feel a lot of pressure when doing something like math problems in our head and probably don't want a friend or spouse to get the impression that we're struggling or even unable to do some of the problems. We know humans will be thinking, "Wow, she's really pretty slow at this task." The dog? He's licking your face saying, "You're wondering whether to give me the chicken or beef, right?" The situation is probably like trying to make a foul shot in basketball in the presence of your friend, spouse, or your dog. Miss the shot and those humans will know you're lousy (even though they'll give you the old "good try" comment). The dog? He'll run after the ball yelling "Throw it to me again! This is fun!"

This topic can be a great one to investigate and report on because no doubt many of your peers have pets. How many of them turn to the animal during troubled times? How many seek solace and comfort in the complete unconditional positive regard provided by the pet? You might also develop a discussion about whether one species of pet is better than another. Many of the studies, for instance, show that dogs are better than cats in providing positive health benefits; cat owners, however, will scoff at you.

PRIMARY REFERENCE
Allen, K. 2003. Are pets a healthy pleasure? The influence of pets on blood pressure. *Current Directions in Psychological Science* 12: 236–39.

ADDITIONAL REFERENCES

Allen, K., J. Blascovich, and W. B. Mendes. 2002. Cardiovascular reactivity and the presence of pets, friends, and spouses: The truth about cats and dogs. *Psychosomatic Medicine* 64: 727–39.

Fine, A. H. 2000. *Handbook on Animal-Assisted Therapy.* San Diego, CA: Academic Press.

Friedman, E., and S. A. Thomas. 1995. Pet ownership, social support, and one-year survival after acute myocardial infarction in the Cardiac Arrhythmia Suppression Trial (CAST). *American Journal of Cardiology* 76: 1213–17.

Obendaal, J. S. 2000. Animal-assisted therapy: Magic or medicine? *Journal of Psychosomatic Research* 49: 275–80.

38
Is Laughter the Best Medicine?

In an earlier entry we talked about how an optimistic outlook can have some positive health benefits. How about heavy doses of laughter along with that optimistic outlook? Nearly everyone believes laughter is good for us. Laughing sure seems to make us feel better, doesn't it, especially when we laugh so hard "it hurts"! Those who laugh certainly seem to be in an optimistic frame of mind; we have already noted how optimists have all sorts of good things going for them, but how about laughter itself?

QUESTION: *If we laugh a lot, do we enhance our physical health?*
RESEARCH ANSWER: *No.*

ANALYSIS

In 1979, in *Anatomy of an Illness*, Norman Cousins preached the benefits of daily bouts of laughter and massive doses of vitamin C in helping him recover from rheumatoid arthritis. If, however, you want to find systematic research showing that laughter has specific benefits on our physical health, you're going to be disappointed. Whether we're talking about measures of how well our immune system is functioning, our tolerance for pain, blood pressure, longevity, or symptoms of illness, the evidence is, as scientists are fond of saying, "equivocally weak and less than convincing." Are we saying laughter is a bummer? Of course not! Everything goes better with a smile and a laugh! As far as good scientific evidence on some of the effects of laughter is concerned, however, here's what you can say when discussing this topic:

- A number of studies show that immune system functioning improves in people after they have been exposed to comedy. Unfortunately, these studies are not usually well-controlled, and the findings could be due to overt laughter, amusement, some other positive emotion, or just general arousal. These studies are promising but much more research is needed.

- Watching a comedy show appears to increase one's pain tolerance, at least for moderate pain levels. What is not clear, however, is whether the effect is due to overt laughter or general physical arousal. For instance, studies show pain tolerance also increases when one watches a show that is really disgusting, scary, or sad.

- Overt laughter does not generally decrease blood pressure. In fact, the opposite usually occurs, at least in the short term; hearty laughter produces a temporary increase in blood pressure.

- Mortality of comedians and humor writers is no different than that of serious entertainers or authors. There is no evidence that having a sense of humor leads to a longer life. In fact, one study suggested the opposite: Having a sense of humor was associated with a shorter life span. Perhaps more cheerful individuals are less likely to take care of themselves.

- Several studies find that people with a sense of humor report fewer symptoms of illness and say they enjoy better health. Closer analysis, however, raises the possibility that these people are simply not overly concerned with or attentive to their biology, and often discount and even ignore certain symptoms of illness.

When reading this summary, it's important to remember that most of the criticisms deal with the quality of the research. There may indeed be beneficial long-term effects of a good belly laugh. The feeling among professionals, however, is that any effect has yet to be strongly demonstrated. We think the best advice here is the same we noted earlier concerning ''exercising'' our brain: Overt laughter may not really enhance our physical health, but let's act like it does and always look for a reason to laugh and enjoy those around us.

PRIMARY REFERENCE

Martin, R. A. 2002. Is laughter the best medicine? Humor, laughter, and physical health. *Current Directions in Psychological Science* 11: 216–20.

ADDITIONAL REFERENCES

Cousins, N. 1979. *Anatomy of an Illness.* New York: Norton.

Fredrickson, B. L. 2000. Cultivating positive emotions to optimize health and well-being. *Prevention and Treatment* 3: 1–26.

Martin, R. A. 2001. Humor, laughter, and physical health: Methodological issues and research findings. *Psychological Bulletin* 127: 504–19.

Martin, R. A., P. Puhlik-Doris, G. Larsen, J. Gray, and K. Weir. 2003. Individual differences in uses of humor and their relation to psychological well-being: Development of the Humor Styles Questionnaire. *Journal of Research in Personality* 37: 48–75.

39
Breast Cancer: Does Attitude Help?

We could show you study after study demonstrating that stress, anxiety, pressure, and pessimism can be bad for our physical health. Stress, for instance, can compromise our body's physical defense systems and makes us more vulnerable to all sorts of physical ailments. Thus, if stress is so damaging to us, it seems obvious we should seek to live less stressful lives and go about our daily existence with a more positive outlook. Be an optimist! Stay positive! Look on the bright side! See the glass as half-full! We have heard it all. But does the positive attitude really work for everything? A good attitude may help with colds and generally provide a boost to our immune system, but are these effects limited?

Interestingly, compared to the effects of negative attitudes, there has been nowhere near the amount of research on the effects of positive attitudes on physical health. Few will deny that a positive approach to life will greatly increase one's psychological functioning, but finding evidence that optimism has a direct effect on our body functioning is hard to come by. There IS evidence showing that a positive life outlook leads to quicker recovery following heart surgery; that such an outlook reduces pain; and that such an outlook is associated with generally better health. But the mechanisms for these links could be numerous.

In this segment we want to look at a specific disorder, breast cancer—certainly a major health problem in the United States. At the turn of the century, the American Cancer Society said that one in eight American women were likely to be stricken. This is also a cancer that understandably has an immense psychological impact relating to self-image, self-esteem, sexual functioning, anxiety, and depression.

Before we bring a victim's attitude into our analysis, let's make an important point. No matter what sort of physical condition we are talking about, from a cold to cancer, one's general psychological attitude is going to influence how one adapts to the condition. Generally, those with a positive attitude are going to cope with a physical affliction much better than those with a negative attitude. Likewise, those with a positive outlook are more likely than their negative counterparts to engage in behaviors that will help any recovery that is possible. But—and this is a big but—will attitude actually affect the biological progression of a disease? So in this case, referring to breast cancer, here's our question:

QUESTION: *Will an optimistic pattern of thinking make recovery from breast cancer more likely?*
RESEARCH ANSWER: *No.*

ANALYSIS

This is a tough call, especially for a couple of psychologists. We firmly believe that psychological states can potentially influence physical ones, especially when those psychological states are negative. But unfortunately, there is simply no consistent evidence showing that psychological processes can influence the actual physical progression or outcome of breast cancer. Robyn Claar and James Blumenthal of the Duke University Medical Center review a variety of studies of women with breast cancer. A typical study will randomly assign victims to either a control group or an intervention group. The intervention will consist of weekly sessions to provide group support, training in relaxation techniques, and therapy to help the victim restructure her thinking about her condition in more positive and optimistic ways. Several of these studies showed positive effects of the intervention, such as improved immune-system functioning, lower rates of depression and anxiety, and reduced pain. But, and here's the huge but, there were no differences in survival rates between the control and intervention groups.

There is solid evidence that an optimistic attitude improves the quality of the cancer patient's life, but there is no trend or overwhelming conclusion supporting a similar link between optimism and disease progression or survival rates. The evidence, therefore, is suggestive and provocative, words researchers love to use; but the evidence is not yet definitive. We should, however, be optimistic and hope that future research will uncover specific psychological strategies that literally help the body rid itself of pathologies, even cancer.

The negative answer to our question should in no way downplay the importance of attitude on one's *adjustment* to disease (or to life in general!). We would never want to suggest such a de-emphasis on the importance of psychological strategies in confronting life's challenges. There is no doubt about the power of optimistic thinking for our personal health. The optimist is likely to see problems and difficulties in life as challenges that can be met and overcome. The optimist is also more likely to be liked by others and to look for explanations behind negative events as external, and not one's personal fault. Optimists blame external circumstances; pessimists blame themselves or "bad luck." This blame translates into personal stress that has negative health consequences. All in all, therefore, whereas optimism may not result in a higher survival rate for breast cancer victims, perhaps victims should act like it does!

PRIMARY REFERENCES

Claar, R. L., and J. A. Blumenthal. 2003. The value of stress-management interventions in life-threatening medical conditions. *Current Directions in Psychological Science* 12: 133–37.

ADDITIONAL REFERENCES

Antoni, M. H., J. M. Lehman, K. M. Kilbourn, A. E. Boyers, J. L. Culver, S. M. Alferi, S. E. Yount, B. A. McGregor, P. L. Arena, S. D. Harris, A. A. Price, and C. S. Carver. 2001. Cognitive-behavioral stress management intervention decreases the prevalence of depression and enhances benefit finding among women under treatment for early stage breast cancer. *Health Psychology* 20: 20–32.

Baum, A., and B. L. Andersen, eds. 2001. *Psychosocial Interventions for Cancer.* Washington, DC: American Psychological Association.

Classen, C., L. D. Butler, C. Koopman, E. Miller, S. DiMiceli, J. Giese-Davis, P. Fobair, R. W. Carlson, H. C. Kraemer, and D. Spiegel. 2001. Supportive-expressive group therapy and distress in patients with metastatic breast cancer. *Archives of General Psychiatry* 58: 494–501.

Compas, B. E., and L. Luecken. 2002. Psychological adjustment to cancer. *Current Directions in Psychological Research* 11: 111–14.

Leucken, L., and B. E. Compas. 2002. Stress, coping, and immune function in breast cancer. *Annals of Behavioral Medicine* 24: 336–44.

Stanton, A. A., S. Danoff-Burg, and C.L. Cameron. 2000. Emotionally expressive coping predicts psychological and physical adjustment to breast cancer. *Journal of Consulting and Clinical Psychology* 68: 875–82.

40
Tragedy Aftermath: Should Counselors Be Available Tomorrow?

Periodically, a traumatic crisis occurs in an organization that potentially affects a large number of people. Examples would be the Columbine and the Virginia Tech shootings. Whenever events like these occur, we always hear or read in the media reports along the lines of "Counselors will be available for the next few days for talking and guidance."

Having mental health professionals available for victims of trauma comes under the general heading of "crisis debriefing." The goal behind this sort of service is that giving victims a chance to talk about their feelings and emotions surrounding the traumatic event may prevent post-traumatic stress disorder (PTSD).

PTSD became a formal diagnostic condition shortly after the Vietnam War, when many veterans returning from combat developed symptoms (panic and anxiety attacks, sleep disturbances, interpersonal difficulties, and avoidance of anything similar to the event) days, weeks, and even months after the stress of combat. Similar conditions can develop in victims following virtually any traumatic event, from robbery and rape to car accidents and being fired. The thinking behind crisis debriefing is that by quickly providing victims with a chance to talk about their emotions and feelings resulting from the trauma, PTSD can be avoided or reduced in intensity. Without such debriefing, unexpressed emotions can fester like an untreated wound and flare up later, causing major psychological difficulties. At least that's the theory.

QUESTION: *Does crisis debriefing work?*
RESEARCH ANSWER: *No.*

ANALYSIS

First, we need to make some points about the aftermath of a traumatic event:

- PTSD is not inevitable following a traumatic event. In fact, research has shown that some types of people are quite vulnerable, but others are very resistant and able to handle trauma quite well.

- Quick, early intervention with victims following a traumatic event is not necessarily helpful in reducing the incidence of PTSD at a later time. Many victims are not "ready" to talk about their feelings immediately after a traumatic event.

- Having an opportunity to "vent" emotions does not necessarily get rid of those emotions. In fact, venting ("let it all out!") of emotions in energetic fashion can actually increase, not decrease, the likelihood of similar emotional expression later.

One method of crisis debriefing involves getting victims together soon after the trauma. For a period of hours, they are instructed to express their thoughts and feelings about the experience. The group is also warned about possible post-traumatic symptoms to watch for as time goes on. Studies of this technique show that it is ineffective and may even cause some harm. That is, some studies show that victims undergoing the debriefing were more likely to develop post-traumatic problems than victims who were not debriefed.

Like a trauma itself, relatively short debriefing that occurs quickly after a traumatic event is probably challenging for the victim to process intellectually and emotionally. Many victims need a period of time, even a week or two, to process psychologically what has occurred, and begin to assess the consequences of the event. Brief discussions with counselors during that processing time will probably be ineffective and may even worsen the impact of the original trauma.

Once the impact and reality of a trauma have been processed and the victim has "stabilized," what steps are effective?

- It is helpful to be around others who have experienced the same or similar traumas. The contact should be in a supportive context where there is open sharing of thoughts and feelings.

- It is helpful to write or voice-record details of the trauma, to get thoughts and feelings out where they can continue to be reworked and processed, again in the presence of others who can relate.

- The trauma can be revisited by physically returning to the place where the event took place. For many victims this step comes only after much preparation and support. The "visit" can also be somewhat symbolic, as is the case when veterans visit war memorials like The Wall commemorating the Vietnam conflict.

Many of these principles, especially the last one, are found in a program Army psychologists are designing to treat Iraq veterans who suffer PTSD. The program involves vivid, realistic virtual reality programs to re-create Iraq battle conditions. Thus, the viewer revisits the traumatic conditions in a safe environment and can begin to restructure thoughts and emotions connected to the original trauma. The virtual reality approach may have wider application for victims of car accidents, traumas like the Virginia Tech murders, and even traumas like divorce or being fired from a job.

Rushing counselors to the scene of a trauma shortly after the event is a well-intentioned strategy. We must not be misled, however, into thinking such a move is going to be helpful in the long run. Recovery from trauma, and avoidance of PTSD, may require more than a quick-fix approach. Unfortunately, in our society, whether we are talking about PTSD, weight control, smoking, anger issues, anxiety and panic attacks, depression, or insomnia, many people look for the quick fix.

PRIMARY REFERENCE

Van Ommeren, M., S. Saxena, and B. Saraceno. 2005. Mental and social health during and after acute emergencies: Emerging consensus? *Bulletin of the World Health Organization* 83: 71–74.

ADDITIONAL REFERENCES

Bracken, P. J., J. E. Giller, and D. Summerfield. 1995 Psychological responses to war and atrocity: The limitations of current concepts. *Social Science and Medicine* 40: 1073–82.

de Jong, J. T., I. H. Komproe, and M. van Ommeren. 2003. Common mental disorders in postconflict settings. *Lancet* 361: 2128–30.

Jones, L., A. Rustemi, M. Shahini, and A. Uka. 2003. Mental health services for war-affected children: Report of a survey in Kosovo. *British Journal of Psychiatry* 183: 540–46.

Mezey, G., and I. Robbins. 2001. Usefulness and validity of post-traumatic stress disorder as a psychiatric category. *British Medical Journal* 323: 561–63.

Weiss, M., B. Saraceno, S. Saxena, and M. van Ommeren. 2003. Mental health in the aftermath of disasters: Consensus and controversy. *Journal of Nervous and Mental Disease* 191: 611–15.

41
Are We All Vulnerable to Post-Traumatic Stress Disorder?

In this section we want to continue our discussion of post-traumatic stress disorder. Do you know someone who has experienced a significant trauma? One difficulty in answering this question is defining the phrase "significant trauma," so let's restrict it to a life-threatening or near life-threatening event directly affecting the person or someone very close. Based on large surveys, researchers estimate that half the population experiences at least one such traumatic event during a lifetime, but less than 10 percent of the population goes on to develop severe PTSD symptoms. In the previous entry (#40), we noted American society's emphasis on crisis debriefing following traumatic events affecting large groups. Given such an emphasis, we might expect the percentage of people suffering PTSD would be much larger than 10 percent. The incidence of PTSD is indeed higher for combat soldiers (somewhere between 15 percent and 30 percent of Iraq War veterans show identifiable signs), but still the majority of combat veterans do not show signs of the disorder. What's going on here? Do media reports tend to exaggerate the incidence of PTSD?

QUESTION: *Are some people relatively immune to PTSD following a personal trauma?*
RESEARCH ANSWER: *Yes.*

ANALYSIS
This is one of those research answers that begs the next question, and we had better be prepared with an answer: Following trauma, why do some people develop PTSD, but not others? Of course, anyone who has studied psychology knows that answering this question is kind of like answering the question, "Why does one person want to be a plumber and another want to be an electrician?" We can, however, make a general attempt to point out some of the factors that make some people relatively protected from the likelihood of PTSD.

- People who have a history of psychiatric disorders in their family, and people who have a personal history of such disorders, are more prone to PTSD. The presence of a childhood trauma leaves one especially vulnerable to PTSD following trauma as an adult. Just as physical injuries leave the body vulnerable to later injury, so too do early psychological scars leave one vulnerable to later stress.

- Some people have oversensitive nervous systems. They respond more intensely to loud noises, pain, and unexpected events. They are more prone to uneasiness and discomfort in new and strange environments. The biological makeup of these people makes them quite vulnerable to the stress of a traumatic event and makes them more likely to suffer symptoms of PTSD.

- Some individuals have formed a rather unrealistic view of the world. They may have lived a relatively sheltered, stress-free, and work-free life, and believe adversity and danger primarily affect others, not them. These folks are ill-prepared for the effective cognitive processing of stress and trauma because their life has been one of avoidance of life problems rather than confrontation and meeting challenges. If a trauma occurs, they react with catastrophic thinking, "My world has ended"—a type of thinking that greatly interferes with recovery.

- Those who have an extensive and supportive social network are generally much better equipped to handle the effects of trauma than are those who feel isolated and lonely. There's no guarantee, of course, that support of others will blunt the adverse effects of trauma because others may try and shield the victim. Ultimately, such protection will backfire; the victim must be prepared to face the trauma squarely, not avoid it. If one is able to face a trauma with the psychological support of others, however, the likelihood of PTSD will be greatly reduced.

- Those who have training in what to do when faced with a specific trauma will obviously fare better. Soldiers undergo extensive training before they are sent into combat; school children have evacuation drills in case of fire or other emergency; some women take courses in self-defense to prepare themselves in case of personal attack. These and other types of preparation will give people a sense of control over the unexpected and will better equip them to face trauma more effectively.

Such research findings suggest that organizations like the armed services might do well to attempt to identify soldiers who are vulnerable to PTSD before sending them into combat. If preliminary tests are developed to identify these soldiers, additional types of training prior to entering the combat zone could be given, or they could be assigned to noncombat roles. In fact, the virtual-reality procedure described in the previous entry holds some promise. Research is needed to determine if such pretraining might provide a psychological inoculation of sorts and make soldiers more resistant to developing PTSD as a result of combat experiences.

One thing is certain: When trauma strikes, PTSD is not inevitable. Many can and do cope effectively with excessive stress and trauma and go on with their lives. It is important for us to reject any message that says exposure to a traumatic event will make us fall apart.

PRIMARY REFERENCE

Ozer, E. J., and D. S. Weiss. 2004. Who develops posttraumatic stress disorder? *Current Directions in Psychological Science* 13: 169–72.

ADDITIONAL REFERENCES

Brewin, C. R., B. Andrews, and J. D. Valentine. 2000. Meta-analysis of risk factors for post-traumatic stress disorder in trauma-exposed adults. *Journal of Consulting and Clinical Psychology* 68: 748–66.

McNally, R. J. 2003. Progress and controversy in the study of posttraumatic stress disorder. *Annual Review of Psychology* 54: 229–52.

Ozer, E. J., S. R. Best, T. L. Lipsey, and D. Weiss. 2003. Predictors of post-traumatic stress disorder and symptoms in adults: A meta-analysis. *Psychological Bulletin* 129: 52–73.

42
Do Long Marriages Improve Physical Health?

You might be wondering if we purposely placed a section dealing with marriage following the section on post-traumatic stress disorder. A divorced person, of course, will say this is where marriage material belongs; a happily married person, on the other hand, will see marriage material as quite out of place here. Keep that distinction in mind as we look at our next topic.

According to national figures, about 50 percent of couples who take on the heavy responsibility of marriage are destined to go separate ways and dissolve their marriage. That high rate of divorce is interesting considering that many studies show marriage contributes to happiness, satisfaction with life, and health. A typical survey comparing married and single folks usually shows that the married ones generally rate themselves as better off physically and psychologically than the single ones. We might ask, therefore, why on earth so many of these happy, healthy, content individuals would be so prone to end their marriage? (One answer may be that only happy couples are around to answer the survey; the unhappy ones are already divorced ... and single again.)

In this section, we want to take a different angle on the "marriage makes for happiness" survey findings. First, we're going to zero in on marriage and physical health, and second, we're going to structure our question around the length of a marriage. After all, if the state of marriage is conducive to happiness and good health, we might expect those effects to grow as the marriage endures over the years.

QUESTION: *Is the longevity of marriage related to our physical health?*
RESEARCH ANSWER: *No.*

ANALYSIS

Obviously, we want to stir up the discussion pot here and raise the possibility that marriage is not the promised land that many of the happiness surveys point toward. Robert Feldman of the University of Massachusetts reviewed a number of studies in this area. His review suggests that whereas marriage can indeed have a very positive effect on many people's lives, being married per se is not the key to happiness and health; the key is the quality of the marriage. That certainly sounds logical, but the fact is many surveys do not convey that message. We're saying, yes, marriage can be a significant contributor to satisfaction and good health if, and this is a big if, the marriage is of good quality. Thus, it is not being married, or the length of a marriage, that is the crucial factor; the defining characteristic of the marriage is its quality. Unfortunately, the quality of many marriages deteriorates quickly. Many studies show a sharp decline in happiness during the first 10 years of marriage. This result is particularly true when the individuals are overly idealistic going into the marriage, or are unprepared psychologically for future responsibilities and realities.

Janice Kiecolt-Glaser and her colleagues at Ohio State University have done extensive work on the effects of marital satisfaction on physical health and the immune system. The effects depend greatly on the quality of the marriage. Couples who are in a low-quality marriage show much greater damage to the immune system when conflicts arise than do couples who face conflict and stressful issues from the context of a relatively stable and satisfying marriage. Also, it is interesting to note that happily married couples show lowered blood pressure when they spend time together; precisely the opposite happens when unhappily married couples spend time together. Once again, it appears we cannot evaluate the effects of length of marriage on health without looking at the quality of the marriage. Simply saying that married people tend to be happier is quite an oversimplification.

This topic, of course, is a good one for generating discussion both in and out of class. Young people are usually very interested in the quality of their parents' relationship. After all, the better that relationship, the more secure the children generally feel. Discussion that focuses on the link between length of a marriage, quality of a marriage, and feelings of well-being among the children of these marriages can prove to be quite interesting and engaging.

PRIMARY REFERENCES

Feldman, R. S. 2006. *Development across the Lifespan*, 4th ed., Upper Saddle River, NJ: Pearson Education.

Kiecolt-Glaser, J., T. J. Loving, J. R. Stowell, W. B. Malarkey, S. Lemeshow, S. L. Dickinson, and R. Glaser, 2005. Hostile marital interactions, proinflammatory cytokine production, and wound healing. *Archives of General Psychiatry* 62: 1377–84.

ADDITIONAL REFERENCES

Booth, A., and P. Amato. 1991. Divorce and psychological stress. *Journal of Health and Social Behavior* 32: 396–407.

Brickman, P., D. Coates, and R. Janoff-Bulman 1978. Lottery winners and accident victims: Is happiness relative? *Journal of Personality and Social Psychology* 36: 917–27.

Lucas, R. E., A. E. Clark, Y. Georgellis, and E. Diener. 2003. Reexamining adaptation and the set point model of happiness: Reactions to changes in marital status. *Journal of Personality and Social Psychology* 84: 527–39.

Simon, R. W. 2002. Revisiting the relationship among gender, marital status, and mental health. *American Journal of Sociology* 107: 1065–96.

43

Does Time Heal the Pain of Divorce?

Material dealing with divorce seems an appropriate follow-up to the previous section! We all know the expression, "Time heals all wounds." Is it true? Does the passage of time have healing powers? Experience often tells us the statement is true. All of us have been rejected or hurt to one degree or another at some point in our lives, and we seem to be able to pick up the pieces eventually and move on. On the other hand, we may know individuals who never quite seem the same after the loss of a significant other, or after some other type of disruptive personal event. We dealt with some of these issues earlier when we talked about post-traumatic stress disorder. In this section, we want to pose a question in the context of divorce, and specifically look at some findings bearing on how people seem to recover from the emotional upheavals usually involved in divorce. We're also going to pose a bonus question dealing with predicting those who are likely to eventually divorce.

QUESTION: *Does the passage of time heal the psychological wounds of divorce?*
RESEARCH ANSWER: *No.*

ANALYSIS

We can hear some of you now: "My friend's folks got divorced five years ago and they've never been happier! When Johnny's mom dumped his worthless father, it was the best thing she ever did for Johnny." No doubt that type of sentiment is true in many cases; there is certainly research showing that people can be amazingly resilient and avoid long-term emotional consequences following painful life events like job loss or being dumped by a lover. But assessing one's specific level of recovery from events can be a tricky proposition, and in many cases one may feel one is "completely back to normal," when that is not precisely the case.

Richard Lucas of Michigan State reports on an 18-year study of German households assessing life satisfaction. Each year during the study, participants were asked to indicate on a simple scale their satisfaction with life. During the course of the study, 817 individuals underwent a divorce. Thus, Lucas ended up with a sizeable sample of people for whom he could compare satisfaction scores both before and after their divorce, with particular emphasis on how well they recovered from the divorce.

As we might expect, for those who divorced, there was a decline in satisfaction scores in the years just before the divorce. Also, following the divorce, satisfaction scores went up. However, even as long as six years after the divorce, satisfaction scores were still not at the level they had been six years before the divorce. Thus, the evidence indicated that recovery from the emotional upheaval of the divorce was at best incomplete over time; the healing power of time was limited. Interestingly, however, for those who eventually remarried, satisfaction scores showed a complete recovery and even went higher than prior to the divorce. Therefore, time per se may not heal completely, but time combined with a remarriage may do so.

BONUS QUESTION: *Are there differences in life satisfaction before marriage between those who will eventually divorce and those who will not?*
RESEARCH ANSWER: *Yes.*

ANALYSIS

Lucas also found that, before marriage, life satisfaction scores for those who would eventually divorce were lower than for those who would remain married during the study. Specifically, those who would remain married showed an increase in satisfaction scores in the four years leading up to the marriage, a boost in scores in the year of the marriage, and then a moderating decline over the next four years, almost back to the original level in the years before the marriage. (We can call this decline the "I-still-love-you-but-the-honeymoon-is-over" effect!)

Compared to those who would remain married, those who would eventually divorce showed significantly lower life satisfaction scores four years before they married. Also, unlike the other group, these eventual divorcers did not show the boost in scores during the marriage year itself. And to add insult to injury, the decline in satisfaction scores over the years after the marriage eventually fell below the scores these people showed four years before they were ever married! Remember, those who would remain married also showed a decline in scores in the years following the marriage, but the scores never fell below the premarriage scores.

Lucas's study contains some definite food for thought, and plenty to generate some fruitful discussion. First, following a divorce, one may not show a complete emotional recovery over time; the passage of time itself is not magical. This finding is consistent with our belief that time per se does little; time allows for other things to happen. As we saw in Lucas's study, one of those things might have been a remarriage. When individuals took such positive proactive steps, life satisfaction seemed to recover completely. Thus, time is not the great healer; the great healer is what we choose to do with our time.

A second interesting element in Lucas's study is the fact that, compared to those who would remain married, those who eventually divorced seemed to be less satisfied with their lives long before they were even married. General life satisfaction, therefore, may be a marker for an increased risk of divorce. When a couple announces their engagement, how often do we or someone else mutter, "This one will never work!" What do we sense when we make such a comment? Are we sensing that one of the couple has a "glass-half-empty" outlook on life and that this outlook does not bode well for something as demanding as a marriage? Are we sensing, perhaps, that one of the couple is using the marriage as a stepping-stone to some happiness level that this person presently does not have? Whatever the case, it appears that general unhappiness with life even years before marriage may be a valuable marker for risk of divorce following marriage.

PRIMARY REFERENCE

Lucas, R. E. 2005. Time does not heal all wounds: A longitudinal study of reaction and adaptation to divorce. *Psychological Science* 16: 945–50.

ADDITIONAL REFERENCES

Booth, A., and P. Amato. 1991. Divorce and psychological stress. *Journal of Health and Social Behavior* 32: 396–407.

Hope, S., B. Rodgers, and C. Power. 1999. Marital status transitions and psychological distress: Longitudinal evidence from a national population sample. *Psychological Medicine* 29: 381–89.

Johnson, D. R., and J. Wu. 2002. An empirical test of crisis, social selection, and role explanations of the relationship between marital disruption and psychological distress: A pooled time-series analysis of four-wave panel data. *Journal of Marriage and the Family* 64: 211–24.

Simon, R. W. 2002. Revisiting the relationship among gender, marital status, and mental health. *American Journal of Sociology* 107: 1065–96.

44
Can TV News Traumatize Us?

In a previous entry, we looked at the influence of video-game violence on behavior, and we also commented a bit on the influence of TV. You'll remember we said that although violent TV content can definitely have an influence on behavior, particularly children's behavior, we still have to consider TV in the context of the larger environment. That is, for some kids, TV is a large part of their life. They immerse themselves in the content, they tend to see programs as real, and they identify with the characters depicted. For these kids, what they watch is likely to have a significant influence on their behavior, and they are likely to imitate what they see. For other kids, however, TV is merely a form of entertainment, and a minor one at that. These kids are more likely to be involved in athletic or family activities, to do homework when inside, and to distinguish the entertainment context of TV shows from reality. These kids will be less influenced by violence on TV.

In this section, we want to pose a question that concerns adult viewers and that relates to coverage of real events on TV. Thus, we're not talking here about fictional shows; we're talking about CNN, MSNBC, FOX, and news coverage on ABC, CBS, and NBC.

QUESTION: *Can saturation coverage of disturbing events like 9/11 traumatize the viewer?*

RESEARCH ANSWER: *Yes.*

ANALYSIS

In 2001, Propper and her associates were teaching a course on sleep and dreaming at a college in the Boston area. The course was already underway, and students had begun recording and documenting their dreams, when the events of 9/11 unfolded. Thus, the researchers had an opportunity to assess trauma themes in dreams both before and after 9/11, and to relate them to amount of TV viewing of the 9/11 coverage.

Anyone over 60 will remember the saturation TV coverage of the Kennedy assassination in 1963. For four days, the networks covered nothing else, and there were no commercial breaks. The content of the coverage, of course, was qualitatively different from that seen 38 years later on 9/11. Compared to 1963, in 2001 there were more vivid images of mass destruction, loss of life, emotional disruptions and upheaval, and potential threat to the viewer.

Analysis of students' dreams before and after 9/11 demonstrated not only that post-9/11 dreams changed significantly compared to pre-9/11 dreams, but also that the dreams could be linked to amount of TV viewing of the horrific events. First of all, after 9/11, dreams contained more threat and danger themes and images, and more negative emotions expressed. More interestingly, these themes, images, and emotions tended to increase as the amount of time watching TV coverage increased. Thus, to the extent that dreaming can reflect efforts to process and resolve trauma and conflict, we can conclude that extensive viewing of TV coverage of the 9/11 events served to increase that trauma and conflict. It is also of particular interest that the students who spent more time talking with friends and relatives about the events of 9/11 did not experience threatening themes and negative emotions in their dreams. This finding, of course, is quite consistent with our observations in a previous entry on the beneficial effects of talking with significant others following a personal trauma.

Propper and her associates believe that the results show how media coverage of an event can negatively affect the emotional well-being of viewers. Reporting an event is one thing; saturating coverage with repeated replays over an extended period of time is quite another. Furthermore, if that coverage makes talking with friends and relatives less likely, then the negative effects of the saturation coverage are greatly compounded.

The next time someone says, "I got so sick and tired of watching the news stories about [whatever], I had to turn it off before I went crazy," you can explain to them why they were wise to do so. Sanity and stability are seldom found by watching news on TV.

PRIMARY REFERENCE

Propper, R. E., R. Stickgold, R. Keeley, and S. D. Christman. 2007. Is television traumatic? Dreams, stress, and media exposure in the aftermath of September 11, 2001. *Psychological Science* 18: 334–40.

ADDITIONAL REFERENCES

Ahearn, J., S. Galea, H. Resnick, and D. Vhahov. 2004. Television images and probable posttraumatic stress disorder after September 11. *The Journal of Nervous and Mental Disease* 192: 217–26.

Hartmann, E., and R. Basile. 2003. Dream imagery becomes more intense after 9/11/01. *Dreaming* 13: 61–66.

Lee, A., M. Isaac, and A. Janca. 2002. Post-traumatic stress disorder and terrorism. *Current Opinion in Psychiatry* 15: 633–37.

Lieht, P., M. R. Mehl, L. C. Summers, and J. W. Pennebaker. 2004. Connecting with others in the midst of stressful upheaval on September 11, 2001. *Applied Nursing Research* 17: 2–9.

Putnam, F. 2002. Televised trauma and viewer PTSD: Implications for prevention. *Psychiatry* 65: 310–12.

PART SIX

ODDS AND ENDS

45
Are Single Folks Treated as Second Class?

Recently, one of our students was sharing her job interview experience with us. One thing that caught our attention was this comment: "I took off my engagement ring before the interview. I didn't want them to know that I was getting married soon." Thirty years ago, such deception was really common; young women didn't want prospective employers to know they were engaged, because that fact would suggest the woman would soon be getting married, pregnant, or soon be moving to another locale following hubby's work. Our clever student might be interested in knowing about a reverse trend that has been documented in American society. To introduce it, let's pose our question.

QUESTION: *Is there a negative stereotype against people who are single?*
RESEARCH ANSWER: *Yes.*

ANALYSIS

Bella DePaulo and Wendy Morris, professors at of the University of California at Santa Barbara and McDaniel College, respectively, have actually proposed a new "ism" for us to think about: *Singlism.* In a nutshell, the term refers to holding negative opinions against folks who are single. There's actually a good bit of evidence in support of singlism. Some studies simply ask subjects to list characteristics that come to mind when thinking about married and single folks. For the single, traits like insecure, lonely, unhappy, immature, uncaring, envious, less well adjusted, and unloving rule the day. Not exactly a complimentary picture! Plus the tendency to hold these negative perceptions increases with age of the single person. That is, a 40-year-old single is rated more poorly than a 20-year-old single. DePaulo and Morris also note a variety of discriminatory practices against singles in our society. They point out inequalities in earnings, benefits, insurance discounts for married couples, and housing discrimination, just to name a few.

Surprised? Many people are. One reason may be that when singlism exists, we really do not seem to be aware of it. Being single is just not mentioned much when people are asked to list groups that are stigmatized in American society. Compared to sexual orientation, body weight, race, and gender, marital status just isn't on the radar screen of most people.

We are reminded of an old TV sitcom from the mid-1960s called *Occasional Wife.* The premise was simple: a single guy had a good job, but his boss was adamant that keeping that job and getting any promotions was contingent on being married. So, single guy makes a deal with single girl who lives in the apartment just below him. He asks her to pretend to be his wife as needed. The idea was to help him cover social events, but naturally the boss would often show up at his apartment. The fire escape made access between the apartments easy, and you can imagine the funny situations that unfolded.

Beneath the comedy, the show's message was clear: Single men, beware! You're out of the mainstream. Interestingly, however, there was no such message for the female lead in the show; she did not need an occasional husband. Betty Friedan and the women's movement had infiltrated the networks by this time! Guy needs girl to advance; girl can advance on her own merits. DePaulo and Morris suggest, however, that in real life we might rate both single characters in negative ways relative to their married counterparts.

One last story about married versus single. One of us was at a Friday happy hour with his spouse. A former student walked in. He lived several hours away and was in town for a business meeting that had concluded. We caught up on the news, including the fact that he had been married for a year (he was 28 at this point). After a brief conversation he said, "Well, gotta go mingle. Ooops! Almost forgot." He removed his wedding ring and put it in his wallet! One can only hope that any unsuspecting lass who perceived him as single gave him the negative stereotype he deserved!

Preparing a paper or presentation on singlism could stimulate interesting discussion on the extent to which bias toward the unattached person could exist in high school and college. Are students without a boyfriend or girlfriend treated differently when it comes to planning social events or being included in group activities?

PRIMARY REFERENCE

DePaulo, B. M., and W. L. Morris. 2006. The unrecognized stereotyping and discrimination against singles. *Current Directions in Psychological Science* 15: 251–54.

ADDITIONAL REFERENCES

Byrne, A., and D. Carr. 2005. Caught in the cultural lag: The stigma of singlehood. *Psychological Inquiry* 16: 84–91.

DePaulo. B. 2006. *Singled Out: How Singles Are Stereotyped, Stigmatized, and Ignored, and Still Live Happily Ever After.* New York: St. Martin's Press.

Zettel, L. A. 2005. Aging alone: Do the social support resources of never-married individuals place them at risk? *Dissertation Abstracts International* 65: 5441B.

46
Rating Beer: Can You Trust Your Tongue?

A number of years ago we published data summarizing a taste test comparing Coke and Pepsi. One particular study asked subjects if they preferred Coke or Pepsi. Then we asked them to "confirm" their preference by taking a taste test. They watched us pour from a standard Coke bottle and from a standard Pepsi bottle before they tasted; the colas in each bottle, however, had been switched. We wanted to see if what the subjects *thought* they were drinking, not what they actually were drinking, played a role in how the cola tasted.

The results showed that a statistically significant number of the Coke drinkers who *thought* they were drinking Coke, but who really were drinking Pepsi, chose the Pepsi as tasting better than the Coke, and vice versa. A few of the participants were not fooled and said something like, "You switched them, didn't you? This stuff in the Coke bottle tastes like my Pepsi to me!" Most of them, however, were influenced by the label on the bottle and said the cola tasted like what they *expected* they were going to be drinking.

One of us considers himself something of a beer connoisseur. In fact, for a number of years he has conducted an informal taste test of various brews from around the world, giving each a score somewhere between 1 (pure poison) to 10 (manna from heaven). Of course, for each taste test, he knew precisely what he was tasting. One afternoon, with the help of a friend, he was able to set up a blind taste test. He was convinced he could distinguish between a brand he had labeled 8 from one he had labeled 5. All visual cues were eliminated, and he

carefully tasted each one, thoroughly rinsing between each taste. After one taste of each, he was unable to make a distinction. Two more tastes led to the same problem; there was no difference in the taste quality of the two beers. So for all you over-21 beer drinkers who have argued about light versus regular beer, and the taste qualities of Miller, Bud, Samuel Adams, Coors, or Yuengling, this question is for you:

QUESTION: *Does expectation influence the taste of beer?*
RESEARCH ANSWER: *Yes.*

ANALYSIS

Researchers created "MIT" beer (Massachusetts Institute of Technology) for use in their study. Actually, the creation involved adding several drops of balsamic vinegar to a glass of Samuel Adams or Budweiser. Most people who taste the new creation agree that the amount added does not make the beer taste worse and may even slightly improve it.

The studies involved a taste comparison of two beers at a local pub and looked at three conditions:

Blind: The participants were not told that vinegar had been added to one of the beers they were tasting.

Before: Prior to tasting the beers, the participants were told which one of them had vinegar added to it.

After: The participants were informed which beer had vinegar added to it, but only after they had tasted the two beers, and before they gave their preference.

The *blind* condition, of course, serves as a nice control condition for any expectations that the tasters have. In this condition they figure they are drinking a standard beer that has not been doctored in any way. In both the *before* and *after* conditions, however, there is an expectation established, an expectation of vinegar in the beer.

In the *blind* condition, MIT beer was rated the highest. In the *before* condition, MIT beer was rated the lowest. When participants were told, before they tasted either beer, which one had vinegar added to it, they rated that beer (MIT) as significantly worse tasting compared to the *blind* group.

This result is not all that surprising. Imagine you sit facing two glasses of beer and you are told, "This one on the left had some drops of vinegar added to it." Your taste buds will probably kick into "blah" mode before you ever taste the beer, just like our Coke drinkers kicked into their "Coke" mode before they tasted the Coke that was actually Pepsi.

What was surprising is what happened in the *after* group. Remember, in this case, you have your two beers sitting in front of you. After sampling each one, but before you give your ratings, you are told, "That one on the left that you just tasted contains some drops of vinegar." Do you kick into your "blah" mode and say, "No wonder it tasted so lousy!"? Apparently not, because the ratings of MIT beer in this condition were not significantly different from the ratings in the *blind* condition. The ratings were, however, significantly higher than the ratings of the MIT beer in the *before* group. In other words, ratings of the doctored beer went down when tasters knew what was going on before tasting, but not when they knew what was going on after tasting. If the beer tasted OK, telling them that it contained vinegar after they tasted it did not make them proceed to rate it as tasting bad. Vinegar in the beer made participants rate it lower only when they knew about the vinegar before tasting.

We imagine nearly all of us have seen some TV show or movie that involves some variation on the following scene: Someone is eating some sort of mystery meat and says, "This stuff is pretty good; what is it?" When the reply is "buffalo brain," there is usually some exaggerated gag response and the person rushes outside to … well, you know.

The study we're reviewing here says that this exaggerated response may not be the typical one after all. In fact, we might expect the person to have perhaps a little grimace at first, but then say, "Really? Hmmm, I wouldn't have thought brains could taste so good!" (The other scene, of course, will be a lot funnier for the audience!)

To summarize, expectations can have a major influence on how things appear to us, but those expectations need to be in place before we have the actual experience. If we have already had the experience, arousing the expectation after the fact will greatly weaken the expectation effect.

PRIMARY REFERENCE

Lee, L., S. Frederick, and D. Ariely. 2006. Try it, you'll like it: The influence of expectation, consumption, and revelation on preferences for beer. *Psychological Science* 17: 1054–58.

ADDITIONAL REFERENCES

Braun, K. A. 1999. Postexperience advertising effects on consumer memory. *Journal of Consumer Research* 25: 319–34.

Olson, J. C., and P. A. Dover. 1978. Cognitive effects of deceptive advertising. *Journal of Marketing Research* 15: 29–38.

Wansink, B., S. B. Park, S. Sonka, and M. Morganosky. 2000. How soy labeling influences preference and taste. *International Food and Agribusiness Management Review* 3: 85–94.
Woolfolk, M. E., W. Castellan, and C. I. Brooks. 1983. Pepsi versus Coke: Labels, not tastes, prevail. *Psychological Reports* 52: 185–86.

47
Do Cell Phones and Driving Mix?

Recently, a student told us a story: "I missed a green light because this nutty woman in front of me was fixing her hair instead of watching the light. I honked, but she just waved at me in the mirror; I think she thought I was someone else. Anyway, I was thinking I wish I had her cell phone number so I could give her a call and tell her cars are for driving, not hairstyling!"

No argument from us, but wait a minute—that student's comment is kind of like criticizing a friend for smoking while we're wolfing down a Big Mac and supersized fries! The kid is going to call the woman from his car to tell her she's not concentrating on her driving? The action kind of begs the question: Are cars a good place for making phone calls? Many folks certainly seem to think so. Most readers have no doubt seen someone driving while talking on the phone; many of you have probably done so yourselves! Is such behavior safe?

The consensus appears to be that using a cell phone while driving is not a good thing and compromises safe handling of the car. Let's point out, however, that the cell-phone safety question really has two aspects. First of all, we can talk about the physical requirements of managing a car. Talking on a cell phone ties up one hand, and that can be a problem. Because of that obvious potential problem, many cars are equipped with a hands-free phone setup; push a button and you're talking with your phone mate, but both hands are still free to operate the car. Even if your car doesn't come with the hands-free arrangement, it's easy to install a system yourself. If we have a hands-free setup, are we safer talking on the phone while driving? That question brings us to the second aspect of the cell-phone safety issue. Is there something about just talking on the phone, even hands free, that compromises safety when driving? This is the safety aspect we want to deal with specifically in this section.

QUESTION: *Do hands-free phone conversations reduce safety when driving?*
RESEARCH ANSWER: *Yes.*

ANALYSIS
David Strayer and Frank Drews of the University of Utah set up a simulated driving condition in their lab. The subjects sat in a fake car and watched a screen in front of them that projected realistic scenes and traffic conditions. Their setup also enabled the experimenters to determine precisely where the subject's eyes were looking on the projection screen while talking (hands free) and driving. In some conditions the hands-free phone conversation began before the car began moving, and in others the phone rang after the car was underway.

In one experiment, participants were tested for their memory of certain roadway signs, pedestrians, billboards, and trucks they had seen during the driving test. Memory scores were lower for those who were engaged in the phone conversation while driving, showing they were not paying attention to important objects relating to driving. Of particular concern, lack of attention occurred whether the object was very important (such as a sign saying children were playing nearby, or a school sign) or relatively unimportant (such as a sign identifying a group as adopters of that highway section).

Another experiment looked at how successfully the participant could navigate the car to a rest area "8 miles down the road." In this study, some drivers were engaged in a phone conversation but others had a passenger sitting next to them conversing with them. Half the participants in the phone condition missed the exit, but only 12 percent of those with the passenger missed the exit. These results suggest that the phone conversation is more distracting than is a conversation with a passenger present in the car. One reason for the difference may be that the passenger conversation often included aspects of the driving task. Thus, that type of conversation was less distracting because it was more easily incorporated into the demands of driving.

If such is the case, we might guess that if a couple of passengers in the car were having a conversation, and not attending to the driver's task, and the driver was trying to get involved in the conversation, that situation might be as disruptive as talking on the phone. Similar dynamics might be involved when several teenagers are crowded in a car; the multitasking demands put on the driver are simply too complex for effective driving. By the same token, if a driver is talking on the phone and the conversation is about the driving task ("Have you come to the red barn yet? Right after that you turn left."), we would expect the phone conversation to have little detrimental effect on driving. These possibilities, of course, need to be tested in controlled experiments.

The bottom line is pretty clear: When a task has nothing to do with the demands of driving (usually the case with a phone conversation, or when several passengers are present), attention from the driving task will be diverted and skill will diminish. Pull over to have the phone conversation—and definitely style your hair at home.

PRIMARY REFERENCE

Strayer, D. L., and F. A. Drews. 2007. Cell-phone-induced driver distraction. *Current Directions in Psychological Science* 16: 128–31.

ADDITIONAL REFERENCES

Levy, J., H. Pashler, and E. Boer. 2006. Central interference in driving: Is there any stopping the psychological refractory period? *Psychological Science* 17: 228–35.

McEvoy, S. P., M. R. Stevenson, A. T. McCartt, M. Woodward, C. Haworth, P. Palamara, and R. Cercarelli. 2005. Role of mobile phones in motor vehicle crashes resulting in hospital attendance: A case-crossover study. *British Medical Journal* 331: 428–33.

Strayer, D. L., F. A. Drews, and D. J. Crouch. 2006. Comparing the cell-phone driver and the drunk driver. *Human Factors* 48: 381–91.

Strayer, D. L., F. A. Drews, and W. A. Johnston. 2003. Cell phone induced failures of visual attention during simulated driving. *Journal of Experimental Psychology: Applied* 9: 23–52.

48
Does Serving Size Affect Consumption?

A few years ago, *The Philadelphia Inquirer* reported on portion sizes of some foods in McDonald's in Philadelphia and Paris. Generally, portions in Philadelphia were substantially larger than those in Paris. Averaged over several items, portion sizes in Philly ran almost 30 percent larger than the portions served in Paris.

Similar discrepancies were found in comparisons of Pizza Hut and Haagen-Dazs ice cream between the two cities.

Differences in portion size are often used to explain what is called the French paradox: How can the French eat foods so high in fat content without showing the weight gains typical of Americans? The answer may partly be found in portion size.

QUESTION: *Does portion size influence how much we eat?*
RESEARCH ANSWER: *Yes.*

ANALYSIS

Andrew Geier and colleagues at the University of Pennsylvania recently reported the results of a snack study conducted at various public places. In one condition, a large bowl of Tootsie Rolls was placed in the lobby of a busy office building. On alternating days, the bowl was filled either with 80 small (3 grams each) Tootsie Rolls, or 20 large (12 grams each) Tootsie Rolls. Note that the total amount was constant across the two conditions. In a second observation, the authors placed one pound of M&Ms in a large bowl at the front desk of an apartment building. A measuring cup was attached to the bowl to scoop out servings. On some days the cup was a tablespoon size, on other days it was four times as large. A third observation was done at the same apartment as the M&M one, but at a different time. In this case, a passerby could choose from a bowl of 60 whole pretzels (3 ounces each), or 120 half-pretzels (1/5 ounce each).

The results were the same for all three conditions: more snacks were selected when the portion size was larger. Selection was based on the total weight consumed in one day's session. It's important to note that in this study, we're saying *selection* was influenced by portion size. The people who were taking the snack

items were not followed to make sure they actually ate them. Of course, because the pretzels and the M&Ms were unwrapped, it is reasonable to assume that the selectors actually consumed them.

Many factors influence our eating behavior, and portion size certainly appears to be an important one. In many situations, it is not easy to leave uneaten food on one's plate. Granted, in a restaurant it is simple to ask for a doggie bag, but occasionally some find even that request difficult. The bottom line, however, is that the authors believe that when we eat, we operate under a *unit bias* approach; we tend to view the unit portion in front of us as the appropriate amount we should eat. That bias, of course, gets a lot of us in trouble with our waistlines!

One unfortunate consequence of the influence of portion size on our food consumption is that in the United States, portion sizes at restaurants tend to be large. Meal size (measured in weight) at McDonald's and Pizza Hut, for instance, is greater in Philadelphia than at the same chains in Paris. Also, ask yourself how often you or your parents need a "doggie bag" after eating at a private restaurant. Restaurants in America love to dish out large servings! The by-product, of course, is a population with two thirds of it members overweight.

One of the great ironies in the United States is that, while we stuff ourselves with large portions, we are bombarded with media messages praising a cultural ideal of thinness. Very often, especially in young girls, this cultural ideal translates itself into an eating disorder. Estimates are that over 30 percent of 9-year-old American girls are worried about being fat and 80 percent have dieted by the age of 13; as many as 64 percent of adult women exhibit symptoms of eating disorders, and even more are dissatisfied with their body shapes. Liposuction and surgical procedures like stomach stapling have exploded in frequency.

Students like to research eating disorders, and it's indeed a hot area. If you do so, make sure you include cultural influences. Eating disorders are rare in many non-Western cultures including China, Singapore, Malaysia, and Hong Kong, but are high and increasing in European countries, Israel, and Australia. Countries with Western values show increasing difficulties with respect to eating appropriately. Why? Researchers point to a "success control" attitude typical of advanced, industrialized societies. This attitude stresses appearance, success, achievement, and striving to be in control. These values can easily express themselves in an exaggerated concern with weight.

PRIMARY REFERENCE

Geier, A. B., P. Rozin, and G. Doros. 2006. Unit bias: A new heuristic that helps explain the effect of portion size on food intake. *Psychological Science* 17: 521–25.

ADDITIONAL REFERENCES

American Psychiatric Association. 2000. Practice Guideline for the Treatment of Patients with Eating Disorders (revision). *American Journal of Psychiatry* 157: 1–39.

Diliberti, N., P. L. Bordi, M. T. Conklin, L. S. Roe, and B. Rolls. 2004. Increased portion size leads to increased energy intake in a restaurant meal. *Obesity Research* 12: 562–68.

Kral, T. V. E., L. S. Roe, and B. J. Rolls. 2004. Combined effects of energy density and portion size on energy intake in women. *American Journal of Clinical Nutrition* 79: 962–68.

Mehler, P. S. 2003. Bulimia nervosa. *New England Journal of Medicine* 349: 875–81.

Miller, M. N., and A. J. Pumariega. 2001. Culture and eating disorders: A historical and cross-cultural review. *Psychiatry* 64: 93–110.

Rolls, B. J. 2003. The supersizing of America: Portion size and the obesity epidemic. *Nutrition Today* 38: 42–53.

Tsai, G., and Gray, J. 2000. The eating disorders inventory among Asian American college women. *Journal of Social Psychology* 140: 527–529.

Wansink, B., J. E. Painter, and J. North. 2005. Bottomless bowls: Why visual cues of portion size may influence food intake. *Obesity Research* 13: 93–100.

49

Is Religion Good for Us?

Now there's a dumb question. Who ever heard of religion being bad? Well, religious belief might be bad for you if that belief encourages you to kill yourself and take others with you! But in this section, we want to ask a more specific question than the one posed as the title; we want to zero in on actual physical health.

QUESTION: *Do religious people enjoy better physical health?*
RESEARCH ANSWER: *Yes.*

ANALYSIS

If you have a strong faith system, you have a leg up on life, at least as far as physical health is concerned. According to studies done by Harold Koenig, a psychiatrist at the Duke University Center for the Study of Religion, Spirituality, and Health, religious faith and practice is strongly related to good health. In his 1999 book, *The Healing Power of Faith*, Koenig notes that those who regularly attend church services, pray, and read scripture:

- Are more likely to have low blood pressure and stronger immune systems.
- Are less likely to suffer depression from stressful life events; when they do get depressed, they are more likely to recover.
- Are hospitalized less often.
- Are more likely to live longer.
- Have a lower incidence of cardiovascular disease and cancer.

Before you decide to run out and praise the Lord, let's analyze this information a bit. It would appear that religious people have these health benefits because their faith system is part of an overall approach to life they have developed over many years, and not necessarily as a conscious attempt to make themselves healthy. We need to keep in mind that sincerely religious people tend to have positive cognitive styles as they go through life. Events in their lives are not perceived as random and accidental, but are seen as part of an overall pattern. Furthermore, bad things are seen more as challenges to be dealt with, not as something beyond their control and potentially devastating.

Religious people tend to give meaning to both good and bad events in their lives. There is an overall pattern that suggests a purpose to life. This view gives religious folks a protective sense of coherence to life. It is also important to note that this sense of coherence increases the likelihood that these folks will engage in health-enhancing behaviors and avoid health-compromising ones.

There's no secret to maximizing the probability of being healthy and feeling good. These states evolve from your physical lifestyle (the behaviors you engage in) and your cognitive lifestyle (the thoughts you maintain each day, and the perceptions and interpretations you make about events and people around you). A sense of coherence and purpose to life, and the confidence to meet the challenges of life, evolve from these lifestyles, and not from antidepressant or anti-anxiety drugs, or any other type of prescription or recreational substance.

Let's also note that one's faith, one's internal compass so to speak, must be real. Merely paying lip service to a Supreme Being just won't cut it. You might go to church so someone will see you there and think more highly of you, but this use of religion to obtain nonspiritual goals will not translate into better physical and psychological health. For a personal faith system to be part of a healthy and productive lifestyle, that faith must be intrinsic; it must be valued for itself, not for the material rewards, status, or power it may bring. Faith that brings good health and a feeling that you can give some control and direction to your life is a faith that is genuine. Such faith will be a principal motivating force in your life and something that influences your everyday behavior and decisions.

Obviously, we can't tell you how to go about finding this intrinsic guiding compass. In fact, if you go looking for it in a conscious way, you'll probably be quite disappointed. Such an intentional search with a concrete goal would be as fruitless as circling a date on a calendar with the notation, "Beginning today, I am going to be happy!" Yeh, right! Good luck! But those who stop looking for some expert to run their lives, stop looking for the artificial chemical crutches, stop being passive and dependent, are more likely to travel a more meaningful and fun-filled road.

PRIMARY REFERENCES

Koenig, H. 1999. *The Healing Power of Faith*. New York: Simon & Schuster.
Koenig, H. G., and H. J. Cohen. 2002. *The Link between Religion and Health: Psychoneuroimmunology and the Faith Factor*. London: Oxford University Press.

ADDITIONAL REFERENCES

Koenig, H., M. McCullough, and D. Larson, D. 2001. *Handbook of Religion and Health*. London: Oxford University Press.
Plante, T. G., B. Saucedo, and C. Rice. 2001. The association between strength of religious faith and coping with daily stress. *Pastoral Psychology* 49: 291–300.
Plante, T. G., Yancey, S., Sherman, A., and Guertin, M. The association between strength of religious faith and psychological functioning. *Pastoral Psychology* 48: 405–12.

50
Will Money Make Us Happy?

We bet most people would quickly volunteer to test out this question. Ask most folks and they will quickly say, "I'd sure love to find out!" There's got to be a catch, though, because even as young children we are told by adults, "Money can't buy happiness." Of course, when they tell us that, we just assume it's a clever ploy on their part to find a reason for not increasing our allowance. Then again, maybe they know something we don't!

QUESTION: *Will having lots of money and material things make me happy?*
RESEARCH ANSWER: *No.*

ANALYSIS

First, let's summarize what we know from the published literature:

- People whose primary motivation in life is to get rich show poorer psychological adjustment than do people who are motivated to serve others.
- People who acquire money and material things quickly adjust to their level of wealth and assume they need more to be happy.
- People feel happier as a result of experiences and activities they perform than by merely possessing things.
- Having money predicts happiness only when we compare people who have sufficient income with those whose income doesn't cover basic needs.
- Big-time lottery winners are no happier a year after winning than they were before winning.

Happiness can be hard to come by. Some people turn to prescription drugs. Antidepressants are sometimes referred to as "happy pills," but we know this description is nonsense. If true, we would all be taking pills. (Actually, sometimes it seems that everyone in America *is* taking some sort of pill! The proliferation and availability of prescription drugs has become a massive exercise in cosmetic psychopharmacology, and a grand hoax on us perpetrated by the pharmaceutical industry! Propose that idea during class discussion and see what sort of reaction you get.)

For many years, we have been fascinated with the observation that many clients in therapy are very unhappy, but they are not clinically depressed or suffering from some other clinical syndrome like anxiety or substance abuse. They simply feel compelled to deal with the fact that they are unhappy. Typically, they are confused about the reasons for problems in their lives that they have tolerated for many years. Unfortunately, many of these folks have been on prescription psychotropic medication for their problem, which the psychiatric profession diagnoses as medical. These clients, however, unhappy but not depressed, do not respond well to medication, and they really do not want to take pills. If they find their way to more psychologically based therapy, we find they tend to be quite open to suggestions and interpretations from therapists about how to confront their problems in nonmedicinal ways. They simply want to be happier, and they begin to see that happiness emerges from what we do, not from what medicines we take.

David Myers of Hope College is an advocate of what is called "positive psychology," and he has studied happiness in America. Among his conclusions:

- Happiness and well-being do not necessarily mean being well-off financially. Up to a particular level of wealth, there is a relationship between happiness and financial well-being; beyond that level of wealth, the relationship disappears. Teenagers from affluent families, for instance, can suffer from anxiety, depression, poor grades, and antisocial behavior.
- Happy people have higher self-esteem and feel more in control of their lives.
- Happy people are optimistic, extraverted, and outgoing.
- Happy people show spiritual and religious commitment, as well as the ability to find meaning and purpose in their lives and events around them.

If there is a common theme among these points, it would be that happiness appears to be something that grows out of things we do, not things we acquire. Reaching out to others, committing to a cause, working hard at a task, persisting in spite of frustration and adversity—these sorts of things seem more related to being happy than merely acquiring something.

Once again, the research is pretty clear on our question, "Does money buy happiness?" Material things are not significantly related to happiness. Wealthy people are only a little happier than those of minimal means. The problem is that when we get money, we just want more; there's always the next level we must attain. We are always comparing our present state to some imagined future state, and when it comes to money, we tend to think we'll be happier when we have more of it. Unfortunately, when we get more, we move on to that troublesome future prediction: If I get more, I'll be happier!

Having money seems to predict happiness only when we compare people who have enough money to those at the poverty level. People without enough money to pay bills or to take family vacations have stress levels high enough to make them unhappy. Big-time lottery winners, however, as we have said, are no happier one year later. Winning the lottery may give them some pleasure, but this event will not permanently change their level of happiness. A lottery winner will possess the same personality characteristics both before and after winning. If the characteristics are related to unhappiness, why should anything change long-term? Think about people who pop an antidepressant for the quick happiness fix. Their personality traits, their basic ways of coping with the world and themselves, will not change and will prove stronger than any pill or lottery payoff. The mood created by the antidepressant pill or by the lottery will fade away. The only thing lottery winners have going for them is that they will be able to afford lots of pills!

Let's take a different slant on our money discussion and extend it to getting anything—a present, a medal, or a plaque. An early childhood memory for many of us is listening to mom or dad explain to us why we shouldn't be constantly asking for presents, or complaining when we're told we can't have that special something. "After all," they tell us, "it's better to give than to receive." That line is one of those stamped into our brains beginning when we're very young; it's right up there with the ever-present, "Finish those peas! Don't you realize there are people starving in [China/India/Africa/North Korea—the country seems to change with the generations]?"

Giving is central to many religions, especially Christianity. An emphasis on serving others, giving rather than receiving as a pathway to heaven, is a common theme. Service to others as a national priority gained much publicity in the early 1960s when President Kennedy spearheaded the formation of the Peace Corps. Some government and civic leaders even suggest that participation for two years in a national service program should be required of all 18-year-olds. Presently, service to others is working its way into high-school curricular options for students, and more and more colleges are incorporating what is called "service learning" into course requirements.

QUESTION: *Psychologically speaking, do we profit more from receiving than from giving?*
RESEARCH ANSWER: *No.*

ANALYSIS

Steven Post of Case Western Reserve School of Medicine reviewed what we know about the relationship between what we can call psychological well-being, and giving and receiving. Not surprisingly, both actions are related to mental health. People who say they get a lot of gifts, attention, and help from others generally show a healthy psychological profile. By the same token, those who say they give a lot of themselves to others through volunteer programs also show good mental health. However, the positive mental benefits appear to be much stronger from giving than from receiving. Providing service to others is associated more with positive mental health than is receiving help.

Much of the research that examines these relationships looks at psychological states such as self-satisfaction, self-esteem, feeling competent, feeling comfort as part of a group, and finding meaning to one's life. Other research, however, looks at biological functioning, like hormone levels that are sensitive to stress, anxiety, loneliness, and sadness. In both cases, whether looking at psychological or biological factors, the action of giving appears to have more healthy benefits than does receiving. In one interesting study, when people watched a video of Mother Theresa tending to the poor, their immune system produced more antibodies that protect against infections than did the immune system of those who watched a more emotionally neutral video. Thus, simple exposure to a giving role model can be helpful to our mental and physical well-being.

Harvard psychologist Dan Gilbert notes that one year after winning the lottery, winners are no happier than are paraplegics one year after their accident. How can that be? When we ask that question, we are forgetting that we are considering the lottery winner and the paraplegic from the perspective of our present state, which probably doesn't include being either a lottery winner or a paraplegic. Thus, winning the lottery looks pretty good and being confined to a wheelchair looks pretty bad. For the people who actually live in those circumstances, however, their current estimates of happiness are seen in comparison to their earlier life and to the anticipated future. The lottery winner is learning that the anticipated effect winning has on happiness is unrealistic, and the paraplegic is learning that many of the challenges imposed by the condition can be met.

The research is pretty clear here, and you can make some great applications and generalizations from this discussion. For instance, consider the emphasis on success and failure in athletics. Success and failure, winning and losing, are great imposters in our lives. What do we mean by imposters? We mean fakes, deceptions, false gods! Winning deceives us into believing that we may be better than we really are; winning can inflate our egos to unrealistic levels, so much so that those around us look for ways to stick pins in us. By the same token, losing deceives us into believing we are incompetent, worthless, weak, and ineffective; losing can make us give up, throw in the towel, and mope around others looking for sympathy and solace. The result, however, is solitude because no one wants to be around the downcast for very long.

PRIMARY REFERENCES

Post, S. G. 2005. Altruism, happiness, and health: It's good to be good. *International Journal of Behavioral Medicine* 12: 66–77.

Van Boven, L, and T. Gilovich. 2003. To do or to have? That is the question. *Journal of Personality and Social Psychology* 85: 1193–202.

ADDITIONAL REFERENCES

Gilbert, D. 2007. *Stumbling on Happiness.* New York: Knopf.

Kesebir, P., and E. Diener. 2008. In pursuit of happiness. *Perspectives on Psychological Science* 3: 117–25.

Larsen, J. T., and A. R. McKibban. 2008. Is happiness having what you want, wanting what you have, or both? *Psychological Science* 19: 371–77.

Meyers, D. 1993. *The Pursuit of Happiness.* New York: Avon Books.

51
Are Weather and Mood Related?

Americans are always looking for a quick fix for their mood states. On December 13, 2006, NBC *Nightly News* reported that 190 million prescriptions are written annually for antidepressant medications. One hundred and ninety million! If these pills are so great, we must be the happiest country in the world (or, more likely, the most drugged country!). We often wonder how many of those prescriptions are tied to the weather. Someone once said that everyone talks about the weather, but no one does anything about it! Actually, this old adage has considerable relevance when the weather is applied to psychological functioning. That is, weather is often related to our mood. In the 1960s, Karen Carpenter sang about how "rainy days and Mondays always get me down." Perhaps you have heard about a more formal application of weather to our mental state, illustrated in the concept of SAD, an acronym for Seasonal Affective Disorder. This depressive disorder hits people in the winter, when there is reduced sunlight.

As if the Christmas holiday season isn't bad enough, SAD comes along when the weather is reminding us of the long winter months ahead (at least for many parts of the country). The winter months can be such a sad time for many people; they're cooped up in the house because it gets cold outside (at least if you live in the north). It gets dark early, and it's tough to take those enjoyable strolls around the neighborhood after dinner; we might as well stay in the house and gain weight (which further depresses us when we look at the scale come January).

We also are more likely to get sick during the winter, and we worry about it. The flu season kicks in around November; and the final insult to our psyches—we go off daylight saving time! Extended darkness really becomes noticeable. When winter comes, many of us in the northern areas also begin to worry about road conditions. We know a woman whose stress level increases greatly beginning in November as she begins to worry about snow and ice on the roads, and how those conditions will make her late to work or even prevent her from getting to work. She worries herself into a real lather with these concerns and gets herself considerably stressed out. And how about all those school delays and cancellations that lead to angst regarding what to do with our children on a snow day? More winter joy!

Some professionals have gone so far to suggest that SAD actually results from this reduced sunlight, which causes real biochemical imbalances in the brain. Thus, a sufferer can treat SAD with exposure to artificial light daily during the winter by sitting in front of a special lamp for a few hours. The idea is to keep your brain bathed in light, maintain an appropriate biochemical balance, and consequently be blessed with a good mood. These special lamps, by the way, can be purchased for several hundred dollars. Obtaining a good "brain tan" is not cheap!

Some researchers note that increased darkness may have an adverse effect on the immune system, at least in animals. A weakened immune system during the winter, of course, could explain why we seem to get sick more often at that time of the year, and why flu season corresponds with the cold, dark winter months. Obviously, if we get sick, we're more likely to feel depressed, so maybe SAD is caused by people worrying they will get sick, on top of all the other changes and stresses that worry us during winter.

On the other hand, maybe SAD need not be such a big deal. Maybe when something like a sunlamp device works, it's no more than a classic placebo effect. That is, someone in the dumps during January believes that sitting in front of this lamp for a couple of hours a day is going to help, and so it does! However, several studies have controlled for placebo effects and still find that the artificial light has positive effects on one's mood, and even affects certain brain chemicals. The beneficial effects of sunlight on our mood states appear to be real in many people.

Brain tans notwithstanding, let's consider a fundamental question about the weather and how we feel. Is there even a relationship between our moods and the weather? We'll give that question a "yes" right away. But given that relationship, let's fine-tune our question a bit, and give you some real ammunition for the class discussion.

QUESTION: *Does the relationship between weather and our mood depend on how we behave?*
RESEARCH ANSWER: *Yes.* Note that what we're suggesting with our question and answer is that winter and reduced sunlight can put us at risk for depression, but we can still spit in winter's face!

ANALYSIS

Matthew Keller, of the Virginia Institute for Psychiatric and Behavioral Genetics, and associates studied young adults and looked for what effects temperature, barometric pressure, and time spent outside have on thinking ability and mood. Temperature and barometric pressure didn't relate to mood unless they were combined with time spent outside. As time outside increased, mood and thinking ability both increased with higher temps and air pressure. (A high barometric pressure is generally associated with sunny, pleasant weather.)

In a second study, the researchers randomly assigned participants to complete tasks either indoors or outdoors. The results showed that when assigned to work outside on warm, sunny days, participants' mood definitely increased; for those assigned to complete tasks inside, however, when pleasant weather conditions prevailed, mood tended to be lower. Thus, the effect of weather seemed to depend on *where the person was working* during particular weather conditions.

In a third study, the researchers looked at the weather effects on mood during two different times of the year: spring and summer (the first two studies were conducted in the spring). Basically, the results showed that the relationship between a positive mood and warm temperature and sunny days was strongest for the springtime.

What is different about a sunny, 85-degree day in early April compared to August? The answer to this question will depend a bit on location, so let's pose it in the context of areas of the country that experience four distinct seasons. First of all, the April day comes after weeks of cold weather that has driven people inside for most of the time. And now, almost overnight, there is opportunity for increased outdoor activities; we do more! In August, of course, we have been active outdoors for months, so there is not the comparison present between this week and what we were doing last week. Sunny days in August have not been preceded by weeks of reduced outdoor activity as they have been in April.

Note the word that keeps popping up here: ACTIVITY. If we think back to our comments on SAD, we are presented with the possibility that many folks develop mood swings in the winter months because they *change their routine* and give in to the darkness. They worry excessively about the dangers imposed by night driving, bad weather driving, flying home for the holidays, becoming snowbound in an airport, getting the flu, or a host of other self-imposed concerns resulting from a negative psychological response to the winter season. Thus, these worriers passively curl up on the couch and give up. They are less likely to go out to dinner and parties, host social events at home, or engage in outdoor hobbies and recreation.

The key to maintaining a good mood during the dark months is to engage in a steady "diet" of activity, just as you do during the summer months. You should schedule special events and activities that you will eagerly anticipate. Sure, you have to bundle up in January to take that walk, but doing so is better than sitting on your butt. One of our wives is a serious walker. She is also a serious winter hater! Still, she never lets the winter weather defeat her when it comes to walking outside. During the winter she spends a good five minutes bundling up in layers of sweat clothes, scarves, and windbreakers. Then, armed with her iPod, out she goes. Her only concession to winter weather is the route she must take. If there is snow on the ground, many of her summer walking paths are just not accessible, so she changes the route accordingly. She always returns home about an hour later moaning and groaning about the evils of winter. But the complaints are for show (she complains after many summer walks, too—usually about the humidity!). Beneath all her protesting, it is obvious she is invigorated and feels good after these winter walks, just as she does after her summer walks.

We think the fundamental idea behind SAD is flawed. As winter approaches and the days get shorter, if you want to believe that you are doomed to get depressed, that's your choice. But remember: *Darkness is not going to make you depressed; it's what you do during the darkness that makes the difference.* The winter months should be viewed as a challenging time to continue with those activities that give you pleasure and a sense of control in your life, not as a time to hibernate! What you do is under your control; the weather is not!

One of our former students tends to get down during the winter months. This student also has a doctorate in psychology and neuroscience, and is well-versed in research bearing on SAD. Here's what she has to say to us, in a letter:

> A lot of rat studies show that brain chemicals do respond to light and dark. Melatonin, for instance, increases in the darkness. And the more melatonin there is, the less serotonin. Reductions in serotonin, of course, have been implicated in depression, and SSRIs [selective serotonin reuptake inhibitors] like Zoloft are designed to increase Serotonin. It's an elegant chemical explanation of SAD. Unfortunately, like many theories, the elegant answer is never quite accurate enough. It ignores what we do! I know I push to keep my exercise habits during the winter. I have a tendency to get depressed during the winter months, so I force myself onto the treadmill, or even into doing outdoor exercise. And when I go outside, I find myself invigorated. It really *is* invigorating to take a walk in the dark, when it's cold, and the snow crunches. It also makes me feel like a warrior woman when I do something like that. Frostbite warnings are no match for me!

We couldn't say it better. If you tend to get down in the dumps during those long winter months and want to purchase one of the expensive lamps to bathe your brain in artificial sunlight, fine; that's up to you. And if you want to really get passive and begin taking antidepressant medication beginning in September ... well, that's your choice, too. We believe, however, you will be much better "inoculated" against winter psychological dangers if you make sure you continue your normal exercise routines during the winter. It also helps to be willing to take on new things, recognizing that the winter months bring special challenges to many other people. Do things for others. Get involved in charity projects during the Christmas season. Volunteer at a homeless shelter during the coldest time of the year. Do things; hit the road; get out there and be with people.

PRIMARY REFERENCE

Keller, M. C., B. L. Fredrickson, O. Ybarra, S. Côté, K. Johnson, J. Mikels, A. Conway, and T. Wager. 2005. A warm heart and a clear head. The contingent effects of weather on mood and cognition. *Psychological Science* 16: 724–31.

ADDITIONAL REFERENCES

Anderson, C. A. 2001. Heat and violence. *Current Directions in Psychological Science* 10: 33–38.

Harmatz, M. G., A. D. Well, C. E. Overtree, K. Y. Kawamura, M. Rosal, and I. S. Ockene. 2000. Seasonal variation of depression and other moods: A longitudinal approach. *Journal of Biological Rhythms* 15: 344–50.

Lambert, G. W., C. Reid, D. M. Kaye, G. L. Jennings, and M. D. Esler. 2002. Effects of sunlight and season on serotonin turnover in the brain. *Lancet* 360: 1840–42.

Rotton, J., and E. G. Cohn. 2000. Violence is curvilinear function of temperature in Dallas: A replication. *Journal of Personality and Social Psychology* 78: 1074–81.

Watson, D. 2000. *Mood and Temperament.* New York: Guilford Press.

52
Does Paper Color Affect Test Performance?

Teachers in college and high school are always on the lookout for ways to prevent cheating by students. One method often used is to print different forms of a test on different paper colors. Thus, if your test is on blue paper and the guy next to you has his on yellow paper, no sense in trying to check out his answer because his question #9 is different from your #9. Well that's just fine and dandy, but the question arises whether the color of the paper somehow makes the test easier or harder.

QUESTION: *Does the color of test paper affect scores on the test?*
RESEARCH ANSWER: *Yes.*

ANALYSIS

This question is quite easy to answer. All a researcher has to do is to give students a test printed on various paper colors, and then compare the scores. If the sample size is large enough, and if the test colors are randomly distributed, differences in abilities and preparation should even out across the various color groups, giving us a good estimate of the effect of paper color on test performance. Nicholas Skinner of the University of Western Ontario conducted just such a study. He gave 265 undergraduates the same test printed on either standard white, blue, red, green, or yellow paper. The tests were multiple-choice and were distributed such that adjacent students always had different colored paper. The results were quite clear: test scores were highest for the test printed on standard white paper. The lowest scores occurred on the green and blue tests, with red and yellow test scores in the middle. These results occurred for both men and women.

What's going on here? Psychologists have long pondered the influence of color on people. Industrial psychologists, for instance, look at color use in the workplace to assess if certain colors might lead to more efficiency. Researchers have also looked at how various colors seem to be associated with producing particular emotional states. Skinner's study looks at how color of a test paper influences how well one translates previous learning from studying for the test to actual test performance.

Any one of a number of factors could be responsible for Skinner's results. White paper, of course, is familiar; perhaps the colored paper proved to be so novel that it was a distraction to the students trying to concentrate on the questions. Maybe the colored paper produced emotional arousal in the students (some sort of subtle anxiety, perhaps?) that made concentration more difficult. Only further research will help determine precisely what's going on.

One thing is for sure: If you're getting low test grades, now you should add a new question to your interrogation list of "why?" After the usual, "Did I study, outline notes, review, ask questions while reading, and so on," now you need to add, "What color was the paper?" If the answer is something other than white, time to give the teacher a call!

PRIMARY REFERENCE

Skinner, N. F. 2004. Differential test performance from differently colored paper: White paper works best. *Teaching of Psychology* 31: 111–12.

ADDITIONAL REFERENCES

Jacobs, K. W., and S. E. Blandino. 1992. Effects of color of paper on which the Profile of Mood States is printed on the psychological state it measures. *Perceptual and Motor Skills* 75: 267–71.

Sinclair, R. C., A. S. Soldat, and M. M. Mark. 1998. Affective cues and processing strategy: Color-coded examination forms influence performance. *Teaching of Psychology* 25: 130–32.

Soldat, A. S., R. C. Sinclair, and M. M. Mark. 1997. Color as an environmental processing cue: External affective cues can directly affect processing strategy without affecting mood. *Social Cognition* 15: 55–71.

53

Hypnosis: Is It Good for Anything?

We're going to give you a two-for-one in this section. That is, we're going to deal with two questions.

QUESTION #1: *If I get hypnotized for my problems, will my life automatically change for the better?*
RESEARCH ANSWER: *No.*

ANALYSIS

When it comes to dealing with stress and other problems in everyday life, many people turn to hypnosis for help. Hypnosis is one of those mysterious things that fascinate most of us. We see movies centered around hypnotic states forcing people to commit a heinous act; we might witness a stage performer make a willing volunteer jump around on stage barking like a dog, or waddling around quacking like a duck selling insurance; we see reenactments of an eyewitness to a crime being able to recall detailed and subtle characteristics of the event; we see advertisements in the newspaper: ''Come to the Holiday Inn this Sunday and be hypnotized. You will never smoke or overeat again! Money back guarantee''; we even see dramatizations of someone put in a deep hypnotic state who regresses to a former life, describing intimate details of events that transpired long before they were born. What's going on here? Just how magical and mystical is this hypnosis thing?

Well, there's really not much magic going on here. The power of hypnosis is simply greatly exaggerated in the movies, in advertisements for smoking and weight control, and in other dramatic stage demonstrations. Simply put, hypnosis refers to a social interaction between two people. One person, the subject, is a highly suggestible type and is someone who is very willing to cooperate and focus attention on what the other person, the hypnotizer, is saying. Consequently, the subject responds quite easily to suggestions made by the hypnotizer. Attention is so focused, and suggestibility is so high, the subject is even willing to tolerate distortions of reality. The subject suspends reality testing and temporarily accepts and follows the hypnotist's suggestions. Remember, however: the subject does NOT lose control over personal behavior; the subject generally maintains a sense of self and what is going on. The subject is not in a sleeplike trance ready to obey any command issued by the hypnotizer.

If you believe you can drive up to the local hotel on Sunday afternoon, fork over your $69.95, be hypnotized, and walk away never to smoke or overeat again, you're under a major misconception. One thing is clear, though: You're looking for some expert to make you better. The problem here is that whatever positive effects we see with this type of hypnosis are largely due to a placebo effect. You want to believe the treatment is going to work, so it does somewhat; unfortunately, the effects are temporary.

The fact of the matter is quite clear: If you want to change some behavior, improve your mood, control your temper, or manage your fears and anxieties—if you want to do any of those things, *you're going to have to work at it!* Sorry! There's no magic bullet.

How can hypnosis help people change their behavior? How do reputable professional therapists use it? Consider the following statements. Do you think they are true or false?

- People cannot lie when under a hypnotic state.
- One should have greater faith in the details of a traumatic personal event when those details are recovered through hypnosis.
- If someone has a memory of a trauma when under hypnosis, but no memory when not hypnotized, then the memory must be accurate.
- Hypnosis can be used to recover memories as far back as the time of birth.
- Hypnosis can be used to recover accurate memories of past lives.

All of these statements are false. If you missed several of them, though, don't feel too bad. One study surveyed 860 therapists about these statements and found that the percentages agreeing with the statements, in the order above, were 15 percent, 47 percent, 31 percent, 51 percent, and 28 percent. Even many experts have many misperceptions about hypnosis.

QUESTION #2: *Can hypnosis help with pain management?*
RESEARCH ANSWER: *Yes.*

ANALYSIS

Ah, ha! All is not lost! This hypnosis stuff is not as bad as we're making it out to be. Just because the technique is often misused and filled with misconceptions, we should not throw out the baby with the bath water. One of the most widely used applications of hypnosis is for pain control, and this area is one that has been studied thoroughly in recent years. Formal evidence from research investigations shows that up to 75 percent of those suffering pain experience relief through hypnotic suggestion. Hypnosis has also been found to be an effective substitute for general anesthesia in some surgical procedures. There are, however, several important things to remember:

- People's "hypnotizability"—psychologists call it "trance capacity"—differs. Basically, that means some people are more suggestible than others and can be hypnotized more easily. It is clear that pain relief is much more likely in people who are at the high end of the hypnotizability or suggestibility scales.
- Hypnosis seems to be more effective with short-term, acute pain than with long-term, chronic pain. There is relief for both types of pain, but it appears to be more pronounced for acute pain. Examples would be the pain associated with labor and childbirth, burns, dental work, headaches, and muscle aches.

- Sufferers must approach the application of hypnosis to pain control with a positive "it will help me" attitude and the determination "to put forth some effort to make it work." People who believe they will always be ineffective in managing pain will not have such determination, which increases the likelihood hypnosis will not work. This type of positive, can-do approach is essential for success in any type of counseling or psychotherapy. People engaged in any type of therapy or counseling are simply wasting their time if they don't believe the procedure will help them, and if they're not willing to work hard to produce a positive result. There are no magic wands; change requires work.

A study by Manning and Wright demonstrates the importance of attitude. They looked at how much pain medication pregnant women used during childbirth. Some women went into the birth experience with very positive attitudes: "I have learned some pain control techniques, and they are going to help me. I'm going to be able to do this with only minimal medication. I'll feel pain, but I can manage it if I remember my training." Other women were not so positive: "Dope me up; I just can't handle pain. These exercises you have taught me are fine, but I know that once the pain sets in, I want a drug!" The results of the study showed that the women with a positive attitude were less likely to request pain medication during labor and delivery.

Let's note one final caution with respect to hypnosis. We are surrounded by certified hypnotherapists, whatever that title means. One should exercise great care and selectivity in choosing a professional to help with pain control. Some professionals, such as psychologists and licensed social workers, undergo rigorous licensing procedures; others do not. The bottom line: We should always seek help from qualified, licensed professionals. And even if they use hypnosis, we should not consider the technique a substitute for conventional medical methods of pain control. Hypnosis can be a useful supplement to medicines, but we must always remember that our attitude and suggestibility make it too unreliable for it to be used as the only treatment.

PRIMARY REFERENCE

Patterson, D. R. 2004. Treating pain with hypnosis. *Current Directions in Psychology* 13: 252–55.

ADDITIONAL REFERENCES

Barber, J. E. 1996. *Hypnosis and Suggestion in the Treatment of Pain: A Clinical Guide.* New York: Norton.

Chaves, J. F. 1993. Hypnosis in pain management. In *Handbook of Clinical Hypnosis*, edited by J. W. Rhue, S. J. Lynn, and I. Kirsch (511–32). Washington, DC: American Psychological Association.

Holroyd, J. 1996. Hypnosis treatment of clinical pain: Understanding why hypnosis is useful. *International Journal of Clinical and Experimental Hypnosis* 44: 33–51.

Manning, M. M., and T. L. Wright. 1983. Self-efficacy expectancies, outcome expectancies, and the persistence of pain control in childbirth. *Journal of Personality and Social Psychology* 45: 421–31.

Patterson, D. R., and M. Jensen. 2003. Hypnosis for clinical pain control. *Psychological Bulletin* 129: 495–521.

PART SEVEN

NOTES FROM THE SHRINK

INTRODUCTION

In this section we want to shift gears a bit. Up to this point, we have considered psychological issues from a research point of view. Whatever question posed, we gave you an answer with solid backing in carefully designed studies. Most psychologists feel that such research is essential to understanding human behavior.

It is important to realize, however, that whereas careful experimentation is the gold standard in psychology, much of our information, theories, and understanding about human behavior comes from analyzing individual case studies. When we venture into the analysis of such case studies, we enter the realm of clinical psychology and the activities of practitioners who spend time assessing, diagnosing, and talking with clients who are troubled with various adjustment problems in their lives.

In this section we want to illustrate some of the essentials of clinical practice. To do so, we will give you some actual case studies from the files of Michael Church, one of the authors of this book. The names of clients, of course, have been changed, and unimportant aspects of the cases are modified to preserve confidentiality. In each case, however, the fundamental dynamics of the cases are maintained. After a case is described, we will pose a "clinical question," and share with you our answer to this question. We will then analyze our answer by presenting our thoughts, analysis, prognosis, and suggestions for further treatment for the individuals described.

As you read through this section, remember the distinction between a psychiatrist and a psychologist. A psychiatrist is a medical doctor, a physician, who has spent four years in medical school and then specialized in applying that medical training to psychological problems. A psychologist has spent about six years in graduate school, learning about human behavior dynamics, how to assess and diagnosis emotional disorders, and how to deliver counseling, not medication, to the sufferer.

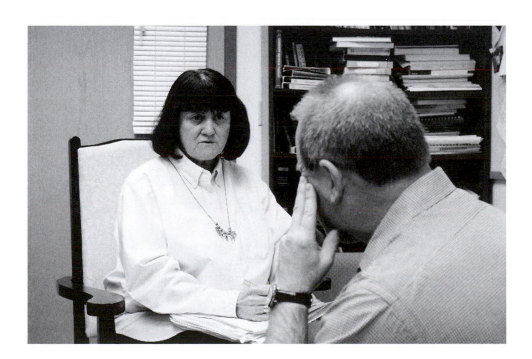

54
Are Good or Bad Events the Best Teachers?

The title of this section sounds like an exercise in masochism, but we want to establish a basic principle of clinical psychology: Virtually all people who experience a psychological disorder are spending a lot of time trying to avoid unpleasant events. This avoidance gets clients into a lot of trouble, psychologically speaking. Before we look at a case study, let's consider a piece of research to set up our discussion.

QUESTION: *Do positive experiences have more powerful effects on us than negative experiences?*
CLINICAL AND RESEARCH ANSWER: *No.*

ANALYSIS
Roy Baumeister of Case Western University and colleagues conclude that the research is clear: Bad events are more powerful than positive ones. For example:

- It is more devastating to lose $1000 than it is pleasant to gain $1000.
- The quality of a marriage is linked more strongly to the presence or absence of negative behaviors than to positive behaviors.
- Sexual problems have a greater effect on marital satisfaction than good sexual functioning.
- With respect to learning, the evidence is overwhelming in favor of unpleasant events. Punishment is simply stronger than reward.
- The bad effects of negative social interactions with others are stronger and last longer than the good effects of positive social interactions.
- Poor health has a strong negative impact on life satisfaction; good health has little influence on how happy we feel.

The lesson we can take from these findings is that trying to avoid unpleasant events can be counterproductive because we can potentially learn a lot more from these events than from events in our comfort zone. For instance, we may be more comfortable avoiding a stressful job interview, but in the long run that interview may teach us a lot about ourselves.

Avoidance of psychological pain is at the core of most psychiatric problems. Furthermore, people who suffer from chronic psychological conditions try to change or control others to avoid pain. The only reasonable alternative is accepting the reality of life while choosing life paths that have meaning and purpose.

QUESTION: *Is acceptance of psychological suffering necessary for personal growth?*
CLINICAL ANSWER: *Yes.*

ANALYSIS
Steven Hayes of the University of Nevada, Reno, has been instrumental in the development of Acceptance and Commitment Therapy (ACT), which proposes we need to accept psychological pain to grow and mature. Many life problems have no perfect solution. Our best option is to accept life, ourselves, and others even when these things can be unpleasant. It is important to remember, however, that this type of acceptance does not mean giving up or quitting. ACT involves adopting a realistic orientation to life that is focused on not avoiding but facing what is

important to us in life. The case that follows is an example of how powerful this type of therapy can be with a motivated client.

CASE STUDY: NANCY

Nancy, a middle-aged woman, came into therapy saying she was depressed and her marriage was failing. She also complained about her pessimistic outlook on life and her dependency on many psychotropic medications. Nancy said her life was pretty stable until 10 years earlier, when one of her children suffered from an accident, both her in-laws died, and her husband had periods of unemployment. The family was forced to move several times as he sought out more stable employment. During this time Nancy began seeing both psychologists and psychiatrists, and was prescribed a "cocktail" of prescription medicines.

When Nancy came to our attention, she learned about the principles of ACT. Within a couple of months, she began to understand that she had been engaging in a futile effort to escape and avoid her difficulties. She began to accept both her past and present psychological suffering, and to realize that her life was pretty good overall. She saw that her guilt over making her family suffer was adding to her burden, and she needed to forgive herself. She worked to develop a clearer sense of her personal values and decide what was important to her now. She realized she was *choosing* to be depressed and pessimistic, instead of appreciating her husband, children, and other positive things in her life.

Nancy decided to become more positive and accepting in her life. Just because she had suffered some personal traumas, she could not expect the corners of her world to be padded for her. She needed to enrich both her marriage and her relationship with her children. No wonder her family members had been avoiding her; she was mired in self-pity, negative-based avoidance behaviors, and dependency on medications. As she became more accepting of her life, and focused on her values and priorities, her husband and children began to spend more time with her; the entire family became mutually involved in everyday activities, discussion, and planning. Before too long she was weaned off all her medications, and she said she felt more alert and more emotionally focused than she had been in years.

PRIMARY REFERENCES

Baumeister, R. F., E. Bratslavsky, C. Finkenauer, and K. Vohs. 2001. Bad is stronger than good. *Review of General Psychology* 5: 323–70.

Gottman, J. 1979. *Marital Interaction.* New York: Academic Press.

Gottman, J. 1994. *Why Marriages Succeed or Fail.* New York: Simon & Schuster.

Hayes, S. C., K. D. Strosahl, and K. G. Wilson. 1999. *Acceptance and Commitment Therapy: An Experimental Approach to Behavior Change.* New York: Guilford Press.

McCarthy, R. W. 1999. Marital style and its effects on sexual desire and functioning. *Journal of Family Psychotherapy* 10: 1–12.

55
Are Psychotropic Medications Overused?

To introduce this section, let's first look at a specific study dealing with panic disorder. Many clients suffering from this disorder automatically want a medication to calm them down and "cure" their attacks.

QUESTION: *In treating panic disorder, is medication more effective than counseling?*
CLINICAL ANSWER: *No.*

ANALYSIS

Some research has been done in this area. Biondi and colleagues, for instance, treated panic disorder with either medication or a combination of cognitive and behavioral counseling therapies. These counseling approaches involved helping clients (a) challenge irrational beliefs, (b) consider alternative explanations for bodily symptoms of panic, (c) face feared situations, (d) practice relaxation exercises, and (e) question the relevance of panic attacks in their lives.

As the study progressed, twice as many clients in the medication condition dropped out. Furthermore, for those who completed the study, the relapse rate was 78 percent for the medication group and 14 percent for the counseling group. The long-term outcome was better for those who came to see that their panic attacks were under their control, and that they could learn to accept and manage their symptoms. Clinical psychologists call this characteristic *self-efficacy*, a perception that one has the ability to meet and overcome obstacles and challenges.

Biondi's work illustrates the main problem with using medications to treat psychological disorders: Positive effects generally do not last. The counseling techniques, however, which help clients restructure their thinking and change their behavior, have much more permanent effects. The principle here is no different than that involved in losing weight: Loss due to dieting or taking pills will be regained; loss due to changing eating habits will be permanent.

Biondi's study of panic attacks raises more general questions about so-called psychotropic medications—compounds used for various emotional and behavioral problems such as depression, anxiety, panic disorder, bipolar disorder, and like conditions. The number of prescriptions written for psychotropics like Zoloft, Lexapro, Paxil, Xanax, BuSpar, Ritalin, and Adderall has skyrocketed in

recent years. Furthermore, the age for which many of these substances are being prescribed has been steadily decreasing, reaching children as young as 6. The use of these medications in the teenage population is nothing short of alarming.

QUESTION: *Are psychotropic medications generally necessary to treat emotional adjustment problems?*
CLINICAL ANSWER: *No.*

ANALYSIS

CASE STUDY: JEN

Navigating through the teen years can be quite a challenge in American society. This is a time when hormones are flying, goals are hazy, and the teen is testing out different social roles in the search for a unified self and personal identity. At the same time, temptations abound from the schoolyard to the Internet. Relations with parents become strained; the teen can become resentful, angry, moody, and unpredictable. Many parents become scared that their child is unstable and needs professional help, and they turn to the mental health system. Unfortunately, this move for help often results in receiving a prescription for a stabilizing psychotropic drug.

Both Jen and her parents felt she had somewhat stronger adjustment problems than her peers. Jen was always an outgoing, active, energetic child. As she entered her teen years, she was quick to question rules and restrictions on her behavior; she showed a hot temper when things didn't go her way. When you combine her search for identity with this outgoing, assertive personality, it's not difficult to imagine that she was a young person who was "noticed" by teachers and was someone her parents worried about. The adults in her life decided she would best profit from medication to calm her down so she would be more manageable.

Jen was born in 1980. Before she was 15, she was a veteran of Ritalin and Zoloft. But it was in 1995 that her true prescription nightmare began. Here's the drug chronology she provided:

2/95–2/96	Zoloft
2/97–8/97	Effexor and Lithium
8/97–10/97	Paxil
9/97–1/98	Zyprexa
10/97–1/98	Wellbutrin
12/97–1/98	Depakote
11/00–8/01	Luvox
11/00–	Clonazepam
8/01–9/01	Effexor
9/01–	Prozac
9/01–	Luvox
9/01–	Zyprexa
9/01–11/01	Geodon

Jen's various diagnoses over the years included Attention Deficit Disorder, Bipolar, Major Depression, Generalized Anxiety Disorder, and Obsessive-Compulsive

Disorder. We guess it's fair to say she had it all (or, just maybe, those diagnoses were less than accurate)!

During her college years Jen experienced a number of difficulties, especially in social areas and in handling conflict in romantic relationships. No wonder! Many of the interpersonal skills she should have been developing earlier were clouded by a prescription-drug brain fog, and she was never able to learn appropriate social behavior patterns.

Jen got into a lot of trouble in college. Her grades were outstanding, but her social behavior was out of control, especially when she drank alcohol, which obviously mixed poorly with her medications. Soon, she was given a hard choice: shape up or find another school! She eventually took hold of her life, helped greatly by an effective psychotherapist she saw during the last 18 months of college.

First, Jen worked on controlling her temper. In this respect, she learned that alcohol made her temper all but unmanageable; she had to stay away from booze! She acknowledged behaving poorly in certain situations that she needed to avoid, like large parties where alcohol flowed freely and people became less inhibited. She slowly and steadily developed listening skills, and began to realize that others often had valid points she should consider before "venting." Finally, she learned she could control a great many things in her life without prescription drugs. In fact, at the time she gave us her "history," she had decided to cleanse her body of the medications. She believed she did not need them to become more assertive in controlling her life, dealing with her problems directly, and managing her emotions better. With the help of her therapist, she *slowly* weaned herself from the drugs. She graduated from college in the requisite four years, has an excellent job in management, and is a happily married working mom. Her life and her behavior are stable, and she is free of all psychotropic medications.

Don't think this case is unusual for a college student. Again and again students say they are taking a particular medication for "psychological" reasons. But when we ask them what the problem is, their reply usually shows some general condition many of us years ago would call "growing pains." Unfortunately, though, they (and their parents) have bought into the message that they can't cope on their own. Many young people believe that they need the chemical crutch and that their problems will magically disappear when they use medication. Some even wear their problems and treatments like some sort of badge.

CASE STUDY: CHRIS

Chris had been taking an antidepressant medication for several years and asked his psychiatrist if it was time to wean himself off the drug. He was also seeing his psychologist once a month and had progressed significantly in many areas, to the point that he was ready to consider living his life without the antidepressant. He had moved out of his parents' house and into his own apartment, gained control of his finances, reduced his social anxieties and phobias, and enhanced his self-esteem. Unpersuaded, the psychiatrist told Chris that he had an imbalance in two neurotransmitters in his brain and that the antidepressant medication would bring one neurotransmitter into balance with another. Thus, not only did the psychiatrist not agree to reduce his medication, but he added a second antidepressant. Chris's psychologist was astonished! He encouraged Chris to seek a second psychiatric opinion.

The new psychiatrist agreed to wean Chris from the antidepressant. More importantly, they had a frank discussion that led to *mutually agreed upon* goals regarding how to handle the medication regimen. This agreement helped Chris continue to make therapeutic progress while lowering his use of medications. Psychiatrists, physicians, and pharmaceutical company advertisements typically tell patients they have a "chemical imbalance" in the brain. The truth is that there is no way to assess whether a person has too much or too little neurotransmitter levels of serotonin, norepinephrine, or dopamine in the brain. Such objectivity is not accurate when it comes to diagnosing the cause of anxiety, depression, and other psychological difficulties. We believe that being told you are depressed because you have a neurotransmitter deficiency is analogous to being told you have a headache because you have an aspirin deficit in your body. You take the aspirin, the imbalance is removed, and the headache goes away. Unfortunately, if the headache is caused by family or school pressures, trying to keep a friend's secret, or some other problem the aspirin is not affecting, your headache will return. By the same token, if depression is caused by an inability to deal with personal difficulties in life, your depression will linger in spite of medication.

PRIMARY REFERENCES

Bakker, A., D. Spinhoven, A. J. L. M. Van Backou, and R. Van Dyck, R. 2002. Relevance of assessment of cognitions during panic attacks in the treatment of panic disorder. *Psychotherapy and Psychosomatics* 71: 158–62.

Biondi, M., and A. Picardi. 2003. Attribution of improvement to medication and increased risk of relapse of panic disorder with agoraphobia. *Psychotherapy and Psychosomatics* 72: 110–11.

56
Can the Alcoholic Drink Responsibly?

QUESTION: *Can an alcoholic learn to drink socially?*

CLINICAL ANSWER: *Define "alcoholic."* We know we're fudging with a wimpy answer, but bear with us as we tackle this complex topic.

ANALYSIS

CASE STUDY: HENRY

Henry, one of our students, returned to college for his tenth reunion. We remembered him not only as a bright student who worked hard for his grades, but also as a student who partied hard and made no bones about it. On several occasions at off-campus social gatherings, events such as senior class socials, the homecoming dance, and other major social occasions, we had a chance to see him in action, so to speak. He was always obviously intoxicated. By 7 P.M. he was "buzzed," as the kids would say, and it was clear he had begun his partying several hours earlier. He wasn't falling-down drunk; but no one would dare get in a car he was driving! Stories about his drinking exploits always circulated among the students and often found their way to us.

In spite of Henry's hard partying style, he always attended our classes, arrived on time, and seemingly was none the worse for wear. If we knew there had been some social event the night before, we might ask him how late the party ran, and he would reply something like, "Oh, I don't know. I think the last folks left around midnight. You know, class night and all that. I'm not sure when I went to bed. Hey! Maybe I didn't!"

At the tenth alumni reunion, one of us was chatting with him, noticed he was drinking soda, and almost jokingly asked him, "What's up with the soda? Give up the sauce?" He proceeded to tell his story.

Henry's parents met in Alcoholics Anonymous when they were both recovering alcoholics. They began dating, fell in love, and married. Dad was 42 and mom was 40. Mom quickly became pregnant and Henry was born normal and healthy.

Henry grew up never seeing his parents take a drink. They maintained their sobriety for the remainder of their lives. Yes, they kept alcohol in the house, and when they entertained they offered alcohol to their guests, but they neither provided a drinking role model for the son nor did they preach to him about the sins of alcohol. When Henry was old enough to understand and the subject of alcohol consumption came up, they willingly told him their stories. They explained they were simply unable to control themselves when it came to alcohol consumption; the booze was simply stronger than they were. As adherents to the 12-step format in AA, they decided they were powerless when it came to booze, and they chose to eliminate it from their lives.

Like many teenagers, Henry soon discovered alcohol for himself. He loved it! He thrived on the intoxicating effects. The "buzz" his friends experienced, the pleasure they felt from alcohol, was experienced a hundredfold in his case. He basically went through high school and college in an alcohol-induced fog. His youth and apparently inherited biochemistry enabled him to function through so-called hangover periods. In fact, he quickly learned that a stiff shot could cure those hangover blues.

Eventually, Henry's booze-infested world came crashing down. He landed a good job out of college, but after about five years his work began to deteriorate. The thing that really brought him down, however, was the damage his drinking was doing to his romantic relationship.

One night Henry arrived at his fiancé's apartment. They were going out to dinner. He had obviously already been drinking (nothing new there!). She told him to sit down at the kitchen table. She put a bottle of booze in the middle of the table, and sat across from him. She looked him squarely in the eye and said, "There's your choice. That bottle or me! Choose one right now. Not just for tonight. Forever! You will walk out the door tonight with one of us, and the other you will eliminate from your life. If you choose the bottle, we are done. If you choose me, you are done drinking. For good."

He had been drinking earlier, but something in her tone, something in her eyes, cut right through the fog and rammed him in his gut like a spear. "I literally had to gasp for air," he said.

"I chose her," he said calmly, pointing at her across the room while taking another sip of soda. "I decided she was more important to me than booze, so I quit. She made it clear to me, no half-way stuff; no social drinking or an occasional beer. She said I just couldn't handle it, so it was all or nothing."

We asked him, "Do you think you could drink socially? Could you exercise control to the point that you could drink in moderation?"

He smiled and said, "My folks would say 'no.' People in AA would say 'no.' I guess I'll never find out. I look around this room and see many of my classmates who abused the hell out of alcohol when in college. Yet, here they are having a couple of beers and then heading home. They made a choice to drink sensibly once out of school, and they could do it. Maybe I have a body chemistry that gives me only one choice."

As a follow-up to Henry's case, consider this story from one of your authors:

> I was a senior in college and visiting my dad and stepmother in Manhattan during a semester break. I was waiting for a friend to arrive; we were going to check out some of the many German bars in the East 86th Street area of Manhattan. My stepmother was a recovering alcoholic (she was dry for the last 30 years of her life), and we got to talking about drinking.
>
> I commented that, when drinking, I wished I could manage to get only to that point of intoxication where I felt really good and was having a good time, but not falling-down drunk; that point where you know if you have just a little more alcohol in your system, you're going to begin acting like an idiot, get sick, and have to be taken home to sleep it off.
>
> I said to her, "If I could just manage to stay at that good-feeling level, right below that point where I lose motor and thought control and throw up—that would be nice." Today, college kids would say, that point where you have a really good "buzz."
>
> My stepmother was looking at me all this time with a totally perplexed expression. "What are you talking about? What level? What's that? There is no such level. Each level of being drunk just says it's time to move on to the next level. There's no ideal, fun level. To have fun you need to get to the next level and keep going and going and going."
>
> Now it was my turn to look confused because she was talking about things way beyond the way my body reacts to alcohol. "Don't you get sick and pass out?" I asked her.
>
> "No," she said, "but I do go into blackouts. I remember waking up one morning thinking it was Sunday. I had begun a heavy round of drinking on Saturday, but now it was Wednesday! I had been living my life in a total blackout condition for four days! I went to work; I partied at night—oh, did I party—but the whole time, my conscious mind was shut down from excessive alcohol. There was no point to reach and maintain. I just kept getting higher and higher, deeper and deeper into the intoxication state."
>
> That conversation convinced me we would never be able to understand each other when it came to the effects of alcohol on our brains; the effects were qualitatively different. I simply did not respond to alcohol the way she did. I would be passed out sick as a dog long before she began her second day of blackout. Sure, alcohol affected the pleasure areas of our brains, and we both enjoyed the sedative, relaxing, intoxicating effects of the drug. But after that point, things were different in our reactions to alcohol. I threw up; she poured herself another drink.

If you're wondering how that evening turned out, by midnight your author (who will remain nameless) was bent over a toilet in one of the beer halls, puking his brains out. (Please remember, this event took place over 40 years ago when he was in college—and over 21.) So much for finding and holding that perfect buzz!

"My buddy and I managed to stumble down 86th Street and reach home. The next morning my stepmom looked at me and said, with a smirk on her face, 'Rough night?'
'Shhh,' I replied, 'My hair hurts!'"

For decades, the question of whether an alcoholic can learn to drink socially has been vigorously debated by psychologists. Some researchers point out the danger in arguing one cannot learn to drink socially, because saying the alcoholic can never learn to consume alcohol in moderation discourages those with drinking problems from ever seeking help. They figure, "What the hell, I can never be helped so why bother to look for help? Set me up again, bartender!" These researchers point out that many treatments for excessive drinking emphasize acquiring controlled drinking patterns to overcome the problem.

Others, however, argue that, like our student friend at the alumni gathering, many alcoholics are biochemically and behaviorally addicted to alcohol; they simply cannot learn to drink in moderation. This position is illustrated in a story one of us heard from an alcoholic:

A recovering alcoholic had been "dry" for 18 years; not a drop of booze had touched his lips during that time. One evening he and his wife were at a dinner party. When dessert was served, he was actively involved in a conversation, and inadvertently ate ice cream covered with crème de menthe. He was half-way through it, immersed in his lively conversation, when his wife noticed and said, "Harry! That's crème de menthe on that ice cream!" Horrified he pushed it away.

A few days later he arrived at home after work with a bottle of crème de menthe and vanilla ice cream in hand, and said to his wife, "You know, that dessert we had last week was pretty good. This stuff is so mild and almost nonalcoholic, I think I want to have it on some ice cream now and then."

Soon it was ice cream with crème de menthe every night, and with an ever-increasing dose of you-know-what covering the ice cream! Then, one night he arrived home with a bottle of wine in hand. He also began making excuses to miss his Alcoholics Anonymous meetings. A slow, but steady, progression of increasing alcohol consumption proceeded until the inevitable happened and he came home early one afternoon totally blitzed!

His wife made frantic calls to their AA support system, and through active and forceful intervention, he was able to overcome this "slip," and regain his recovery status. He learned a hard lesson: no consumption of alcohol was possible in his case; for whatever reason, his only option was complete abstinence.

Our clinical experience has taught us that the most reasonable answer to the question posed at the beginning of this section *depends* on the type of drinker. We have seen chronic drinkers who show they cannot drink in a controlled or social way. They drink too much and too often over a long period of time. We have also worked with alcohol abusers who recognize they have a problem and are motivated to learn ways to control their consumption. We find these clients can use psychological principles to moderate their drinking, just as others can learn to gamble, use the Internet, or eat in moderation.

The application of fundamental psychological principles of learning to the control of behavior is a great topic for a paper. The alcohol abuser, for instance, can (a) restrict drinking to weekends or a certain time of day, (b) maintain an absolute limit to the amount consumed, (c) never drink when driving or caring for children, (d) examine the situations that encourage inappropriate drinking, and so on. These are all examples of applying basic learning principles to behavior, and they apply to any type of behavior.

To summarize, remember Henry who referred to his classmates who partied hard in college, but now showed more responsible drinking patterns? Unlike them, for Henry, controlled drinking is not an option. Perhaps we need to distinguish between *abusers* and *alcoholics*. The abusers can get trapped in behavior patterns of excessive drinking and need help to break those patterns and restrict alcohol consumption. The alcoholic can never learn moderate drinking and must be encouraged to abstain.

Researchers will continue to present evidence, both pro and con, on the question of whether the alcoholic can learn to drink socially. As a final note, however, it can be argued that the question is irrelevant. If someone has a problem with alcohol abuse, why would that person want to control the problem only partially and try to learn moderate consumption? As long as there is a chance of "slipping" out of the moderation, why take a chance? The prudent position is to recognize, "I can control my behavior and my thinking except when I am drinking. I resolve, therefore, to take better control of my life and abstain from alcohol entirely." Abstinence puts any excessive drinker, alcoholic or nonalcoholic (however one chooses to define those terms), on safer ground.

PRIMARY REFERENCES

Commentaries on Sobell and Sobell 1995. *Addiction* 90: 1157–97.

Sobell, M. B., and L. C. Sobell. 1995. Controlled drinking after 25 years. (Editorial) *Addiction* 90: 1149–53.

Vannicelli, M. 2002. A dualistic model for group treatment of alcohol problems: Abstinence-based treatment for alcoholics, moderation training for problem drinkers. *International Journal of Group Psychotherapy* 52: 189–213.

ADDITIONAL REFERENCES

Drewery, J. 1974. Social drinking as a therapeutic goal in the treatment of alcohol. *Alcohol and Alcoholism* 9: 43–47.

Marlattt, G. G. 1998. *Harm Reduction: Pragmatic Strategies for Managing High Risk Behaviors.* New York: Guilford Press.

Royce, J. E., and D. Scratchley. 1996. *Alcohol and Alcohol Problems.* New York: Simon & Schuster.

57
Should Couples Go to Marital Counseling Together?

QUESTION: *When dealing with marital problems, is it necessary for both individuals comprising the couple to attend therapeutic sessions.*

CLINICAL ANSWER: *No.*

ANALYSIS

Our experiences with marital counseling have shown that joint sessions are some-times inadvisable and unnecessary.

- Some spouses are simply too defensive or do not want to give up feelings of control.
- Many couples respond poorly to the open communication in marital counseling.
- Some individuals do not believe that they or the partner can change.

Remember that marriage is a system and that change in either member will put pressure on the partner to adapt. The adaptation will either help or hurt the system. If the partner who is the target of the changes is motivated to help the system survive, the couple is likely to adapt.

CASE STUDY: PHIL AND MARILYN

Phil was in great distress. He was unhappy with his wife, Marilyn, whom he said was crude, drank too much, and made little effort to make him feel desired or desirable. Marilyn also refused to join him in therapy.

Phil's therapist told him to focus on what he could directly control, which, of course, did not include his wife's behavior. Even though her behavior was the source of his dissatisfaction, he had to realize he could not control her. He needed to make constructive changes in his life, changes that would force her to adapt (or not!) and behave in more appropriate ways.

For example, Phil complained that when they went out with friends, Marilyn typically drank too much and made him the butt of crude and tasteless jokes. He told her these behaviors made him uncomfortable, but his protests had no effect. During therapy, Phil considered an alternative approach to the problem: The next time they went out with friends, if Marilyn behaved in her typically crude fashion, Phil would politely excuse himself and go home. He had to be prepared, of course, to carry out this threat, so he should remember to take taxi fare or the spare car keys with him!

It wasn't long before Phil and Marilyn were out with friends. She drank too much and began telling belittling jokes aimed at him. He suddenly got up and announced he would no longer tolerate her behavior. He left the restaurant and drove off in their car, leaving her to find her own way home.

Marilyn was genuinely embarrassed and realized Phil was serious about her behavior, and was prepared to respond. Notice that Phil had put responsibility for changing her behavior in her hands, where it belonged, not in his.

In therapy, Phil worked on other strategies for other situations. Marilyn began to show she cared enough for him and their marriage by adapting and changing. She drastically curtailed her drinking and crudeness. Their relationship did not become transformed into a fairy tale romance made in heaven, but it dramatically improved. Note that Marilyn never set foot in the therapist's office.

58

Can Attention Serve as a Powerful Reward?

Attention is an extremely powerful reinforcer for both children and adults. We often underestimate its power because it isn't as obvious as money, medals, awards, or other tangible reinforcers. Nevertheless, we have found in both clinical and personal experiences that attention can be used to change even rigidly entrenched behavioral patterns.

QUESTION: *Can attention be used to change behavior that is well learned, habitual, and self-damaging?*

CLINICAL ANSWER: *Yes.*

ANALYSIS

CASE STUDY: SALLY

Sally's case illustrates the power of attention in dealing with a childhood problem. Sally's parents brought the 8-year-old in for therapy because she was having difficulty with normal bowel movements. It was not uncommon for her to be constipated for four to five days. The parents had tried many approaches to handling this issue, but all had failed.

Their pediatrician told them that structural problems in the colon and rectum could occur in the future if the situation did not change. To complicate matters, Sally was terrified of having a bowel movement at school because she once caused an overflow of the plumbing, which led to taunting from her peers and deep embarrassment for her.

The therapeutic strategy adopted for Sally made use of basic behavioral principles. Typically, Sally went outside and played with her friends right after school, and sometimes she had "accidents" in her pants when active. To avoid this situation, her mom was told to make sure that, each day after school, Sally sit on the toilet for one half hour whether or not she felt like "going." The therapist hoped that sitting on the toilet would prompt her to have a bowel movement, as the toilet seat was an important stimulus for such behavior, especially if she had not gone for a day or two. If she was successful, she could immediately go out and play.

Note how this regimen used playtime and attention from friends as a reward for sitting on the toilet and/or having a bowel movement. Sally wanted to play with her friends after school; this was an important time for her. Because attention from friends was more pleasurable than sitting alone on the toilet, a successful bowel movement could be reinforced by going outside to play much sooner. This result is exactly what happened. Within a few weeks she was "regular."

Successful bowel movements were also accompanied by parental praise. Praise is a type of attention and is generally a positive technique parents can use effectively with children. Psychologists have researched the use of social praise and have found it is helpful to praise children's efforts, especially on difficult tasks. Like anything else, however, praise should be in appropriate amounts; excessive praise for children's efforts may lead them to believe that they have little ability on that skill. We do not want children to become overly dependent on our approval. As they mature, they need to take more responsibility in evaluating their own performance.

59

Should We Spend Time Asking "Why"?

We want to end our brief journey into clinical psychology by dealing with a misunderstanding about counseling and helping people. Many students think that psychologists spend most of their time with clients asking "why" they are troubled. Many students also feel the answer requires an intense investigation of the client's past, particularly their childhood. The fact is, asking "Why?" and investigating one's past are not the essence of the clinical psychology process.

QUESTION: *When confronting negative emotions, does asking, "Why do I feel this way?" necessarily produce insight and growth?*
CLINICAL ANSWER: *No.*

ANALYSIS

We all experience negative emotions, and learning to confront them is a key aspect of most forms of counseling. Most people go into counseling seeking an answer to the question: "Why I am feeling this way? Why do I have these negative emotional states?" Common sense says answering the question should lead to greater insight, learning, understanding, and positive growth. Research, however, says seeking an answer can be unproductive and even harmful.

Ethan Kross of Columbia University and colleagues asked undergraduate students to recall an experience when they felt intense anger toward someone. Later, one group of students (*self-immersed*) vividly reflected on the experience in their minds, actually trying to relive the experience. Students in a second group (*self-distanced*) reflected on the experience, but imagined they were watching it unfold as an objective observer.

While reflecting on the experience, either from an *immersed* or a *distanced* perspective, all students focused on the precise emotions they were feeling (a *what* focus), or on the reasons behind their feelings (a *why* focus). After the reflection exercise, all students indicated the level of anger they were feeling about the original experience.

The results showed that taking a *why* approach lowered anger levels, but only for the students in the *self-distanced* condition. In fact, the *why/self-distanced* condition was the only condition that showed reduced levels of anger when thinking about the original experience.

The lesson is clear: Dwelling on "Why do I feel this way?" is not effective unless clients are able to view themselves and others more objectively. Thus, counseling strategies should focus on helping clients restructure their thinking about themselves and others; on understanding that control is best exercised on themselves and not on others; and on understanding that positive growth requires posing not the question of "Why?" but the question of "What can I do to develop patterns of thinking and behavior that bring me more satisfying outcomes?" These lessons from the world of clinical psychology, of course, certainly apply to our everyday activities.

PRIMARY REFERENCES

Kross, E., O. Ayduk, and W. Mischel. 2005. When asking "Why" does not hurt: Distinguishing rumination from reflective processing of negative emotions. *Psychological Science* 16: 709–15.

Nofen-Hoeksema, S. 1991. Responses in depression and their effects on the duration of depressive episodes. *Journal of Abnormal Psychology* 100: 569–82.

Teasdale, J. D. 1988. Cognitive vulnerability to persistent depression. *Cognition and Emotion* 2: 247–74.

BIBLIOGRAPHY

Buunk, A. P., and M. Van Vugt. 2007. *Applying Social Psychology: From Problem to Solution.* Thousand Oaks, CA: Sage Publications. This book offers a clear guide to help students apply social-psychological theory to everyday situations. The book shows students how to define a problem and design a research project to test hypotheses.

Carson, D., R. Milne, F. Pakes, K. Shaley, and A. Shawyer, eds. 2007. *Applying Psychology to Criminal Justice.* New York: John Wiley & Sons. This book is edited by four psychologists and a lawyer and provides examples of how psychology can be applied to various areas of the criminal justice system.

Kazdin, A. E., ed. *Encyclopedia of Psychology.* 2000. New York: Oxford University Press. This 8-volume set was co-published by the American Psychological Association and by Oxford University Press. Content can be accessed through the database Psyc-BOOKS (see "Research Databases" in this bibliography).

Mook, D. 2004. *Classic Experiments in Psychology.* Westport, CT: Greenwood Publishing. The author provides an in-depth, college-level analysis of classic psychological experiments and their implications. This book will broaden students' understanding of psychological research and develop a better feel for how to translate practical issues into testable hypotheses.

Robinson-Riegler, B., and G. Robinson-Riegler. 2007. *Cognitive Psychology: Applying the Science of the Mind.* New York: Allyn & Bacon. This book covers the application of cognitive psychology to issues in everyday life. The author provides illustrations of the everyday relevance of research in the areas of thinking, memory, consciousness, perception, language, and attention.

Strongman, K. T. 2006. *Applying Psychology to Everyday Life: A Beginner's Guide.* New York: John Wiley & Sons. This textbook offers an introduction to basic psychological concepts and provides a practical analysis of questions and issues that can make a difference in the real world.

RESEARCH DATABASES
Books in Print
http://www.booksinprint.com/bip. Lists titles from North American publishers.

PsycARTICLES
http://www.apa.org/psycarticles. A full-text database of more than 50 psychology journals. Published by the American Psychological Association.

PsycBOOKS
http://www.apa.org/psycbooks. Full-text articles of book chapters, including entries from the *Encyclopedia of Psychology.* Published by the American Psychological Association.

PsycINFO

http://www.apa.org/psycinfo. American Psychological Association index to research in psychology and related fields. Provides abstract and index database of scholarly books, journals, and dissertations.

WEBSITES

American Psychological Association
http://www.apa.org/

Association for Psychological Science
http://www.psychologicalscience.org/

INDEX

About the Author

CHARLES I. BROOKS is Professor and Chair of the Department of Psychology, King's Collge, Wilkes-Barre, Pennsylvania. He received his bachelor's degree in psychology from Duke University, his master's in psychology from Wake Forest University, and his doctorate in experimental psychology from Syracuse University. He has taught at King's College since 1975 and was designated a distinguished service professor in 1993. He has authored or co-authored more than 40 scholarly publications in psychology.

MICHAEL A. CHURCH is Associate Professor of Psychology at King's College in Wilkes-Barre, Pennsylvania. He received his bachelor's degree in psychology from California State University at Fullerton, and his master's and doctoral degrees in psychology from the University of Miami. He has taught at King's College since 1976, and has been a licensed clinical psychologist with a private practice since 1980. He is a member of the Council of National Register of Health Service Providers in Psychology.